SPHERE COLOUR

CW00450215

FRUIT AND VEGETABLES

SPHERE BOOKS LIMITED
London and Sydney

CONTENTS

Production: Inmerc BV, Wormer, Holland, and Mercurius UK
Limited, 11 East Stockwell Street, Colchester, Essex
Text: Tony Loynes
Photo Cover: Harry Photographic Agency
Layout: Inmerc BV
Typesetting: RCO/Telezet BV, Velp
Printing: BV Kunstdrukkerij Mercurius-Wormerveer, Holland
This edition published by Sphere Books Ltd., London 1984

SPHERE

© 1985 Mercbook International Ltd., Guernsey

INTRODUCTION

Just as a garden full of the colour and fragrance of flowers appeals to the heart and mind of the gardener, a flourishing plot of fruit and vegetables brings its own, more basic, attractions: to the stomach and pocket.

But there is something far more rewarding about growing one's own produce than the undeniable delight of a supply of cheap, fresh fruit and vegetables. Take a stroll into the garden on a summer's evening and pick juicy, ripe strawberries or crisp, sweet, bursting pea pods. You will experience the joy that comes from having been involved in the whole process from beginning to end. The satisfaction is far greater than simply being able to thumb your nose at the local greengrocer, and cannot be measured in mere cash terms.

But is the prospect of cheap, fresh fruit and vegetables within reach of us all? Doesn't it require skills, expensive tools and a considerable investment in time and effort to grow one's own produce? Obviously, no well-run garden providing a supply of produce is going to spring up overnight. But no special skills are needed and the knowledge you require is available in this book. All you need are a few basic tools and the motivation. Whether this comes from pressing economic reasons or from the desire to better utilise that patch of land lying un-used outside the back door, it's a safe bet that once you have enjoyed your first crop, and discovered how tasty fresh, home-grown, produce is you will be hooked. No hobby you could choose is more rewarding than cultivating fruit and vegetables. At its most basic it fulfils the need to eat well and economically, but it also satisfies the desire in all of us to do something creative. It provides healthy exercise, fresh air and an absorbing interest. It enables the gardener to be at one with his own patch of land – charting the seasons and the changing needs of his plot, preparing, feeding, nurturing, cultivating... and finally reaping the rewards.

A garden is difficult to ignore and some work is necessary if it is not to become an unattractive jungle of weeds. With a little extra effort you could have an absorbing hobby and a rewarding supply of produce. As this book will show, even a small plot of land can provide a very useful supply if careful selection is made of crops and the information given is followed properly. Gardening can be an all-consuming hobby, demanding enormous amounts of time and effort from the devoted gardener. But it need not be. There are, of course, basic tasks to be carried out in any garden but those with less time to devote should not be put off by the idea that it involves too great a commit-

INTRODUCTION

ment. A modest investment of time and effort, applied to a manageable-sized plot, can still bring significant results. Be realistic. The busy man or woman will not be capable of managing the sort of garden with which an enthusiastic retired person may cope. If gardening is to remain an enjoyable hobby, rather than a chore, do not take on more than you can reasonably handle. Why not start small and build up to cultivating a larger area when you know how much you can manage. Gardening books frequently refer to having 'green fingers', implying that gardening is a skill secretly acquired and transmitted to the soil and plants through magic hands. Not so! If the phrase means anything it suggests that the more one studies and practices the art, the more in tune one becomes with nature, the changing seasons and the needs of the soil and your plants. But all this can be learned both logically and instinctively and comes with practice. It is not conferred selectively by a god of the garden, excluding some from its mysteries forever and bestowing magical powers on others.

At its simplest, and gardening should always be simple, it is a matter of following a series of straightforward steps and applying some common sense. If you can provide the latter then this book should supply the rest.

In the following chapters we will be telling you all you need to know about your garden. The chapter on preparing the ground deals with the various soil types, how to improve your soil and how to get the best out of your crops.

In succeeding chapters we explain how to plan your garden, where best to plant and sow certain crops, how to rotate your crops to get the best from the soil and how to select your tools. There is all you need to know about sowing seeds, about grafting and replanting and we tell you what important steps to take during the growing season to ensure you get the best crop. During the growing season your crops will come under attack, unless you are lucky, from pests and disease. Many of these are easy to treat, others will require greater attention and we explain the causes and remedies so you can protect the crops you have worked so hard to produce. Our chapter on preserving, including advice on freezing, will be a great help, to those who grow an extra supply to enjoy throughout the year.

A major part of this book contains our full colour photograph section. This is a comprehensive, detailed index of fruit and vegetables giving valuable information on cultivation, care, harvesting and preserving, in addition to a full general description.

PREPARING THE GROUND

Success in growing your own fruit and vegetables depends entirely on the quality of your soil.

We've all heard despairing gardeners moan about their soil as though there is little that can be done with poor quality raw materials. This is not true, and what is more there are various types of fruit and vegetables that can thrive in soils not normally regarded as the best.

Almost all soil types, with the exception of the very worst, can be considerably improved. You will, however, have to identify your soil type before you can set about improving it. Soils generally fall into one of five main categories: peat, sand, loam, chalk and clay. Most gardens will have a mixture with one type predominating. Soils are classified according to the amount of acid or alkali in them. The acidity of the soil is governed by the amount of lime it contains. A soil rich in lime or chalk is alkaline; without these elements it is acidic. The measurement of acidity or alkalinity is done on the pH scale which is graded from 0-14. Above 7 a soil is alkaline and below 6.5 it is acidic. Ideally for your plants a soil should have a pH reading of around 7.

So how do you identify your soil type? Here is a description of the five main categories.

Clay. The soil particles are small and cling together making drainage poor and cultivation difficult. Soils are normally wet and sticky, heavy to work and often impossible in rainy spells. The growing season in clay soils is often shortened because sowing has to be delayed until the soil is dryer and warmer. Though there are problems with clay soil it does have advantages in that it doesn't dry out as quickly in summer and, when well worked, it can produce heavy and good quality crops. Clay soil especially suits brassicas, beans, peas, potatoes, salads and soft fruits. The addition of organic matter greatly improves clay soil and the addition of lime will help, allowing particles to bind together more so that air and water can pass through.

Sand. Easy to work and quick to warm in the spring, sandy soils are splendid for growing early crops. The problem, however, is that they drain so rapidly that all the goodness tends to be washed out of them. Sandy soil can be recognised by squeezing it between the fingers. It does not bind together well and looks and feels rough. Loss of nutrients in sandy soil – called 'leaching' – can be treated by digging in compost or well-rotted manure. The resulting humus which is formed helps to retain moisture and thus nutrients. Sandy soils are frequently deficient in potash, and sulphate of potash, in addition to a general fertiliser,

may need to be added at 1 oz per square yard. Well-cultivated sandy soils are good for root crops, onions, asparagus, potatoes, tomatoes and half-hardy tree fruits like apricot and peach.

Peat. This type of soil, made up of part-decomposed matter, is the least common in the garden and is inclined to be acidic and poor in draining. In the more serious cases some

form of added drainage may have to be dug in, and in most cases the addition of a lime nutrient and either course sand or weathered ashes will be needed. While you are improving the quality of the soil it would be best to concentrate on crops which do well in acidic or neutral soils, like potatoes.

Chalk. Chalk subsoil is usually hidden by a thin layer of topsoil but is easily identifiable, especially when wet, since the chalk sticks to the heels. Strongly alkaline, the main need with chalk soils is for organic manure. Dig in good garden compost or manure in autumn or early winter. Chalky soil dries out quickly and some years, especially when dry, will need watering and mulching. When well cultivated chalky soils suit most types of vegetables, with the exception of potatoes, and most stone fruits.

Loam. This is the best type of soil to have and anyone whose garden is blessed with loamy soil is almost committing an offence if he does not cultivate it. Loamy soil is a mixture of sand and clay and is splendidly fertile. Easy to cultivate, it retains moisture and nutrients and yet, at the same time, drains well.

Manuring

There are many materials, both organic and inorganic, that can be used to improve the quality of your soil and to promote the better growth of your plants. Humus is most important in the soil since it helps with water retention and thus to keep nutrients in the soil. Most plants will thrive if your soil has been dressed with a good well-rotted compost. Other organic treatments which will benefit the soil include: animal manure which must be well-rotted or it can be harmful, used mush-room compost sold off by mushroom growers which is good for all but lime-hating plants, seaweed which is rich in nutrients like potash and pulverised bark which can be used as a good all-purpose mulch.

If your pH reading is unfavourable, however, you may need to adjust the acidity or alkalinity. Soil with a pH balance below the ideal level of around 7 inhibits the uptake of important nutrients. Small additions of hydrated lime are the most effective treatment. Simple ground limestone or chalk can also be used. It is much more difficult to alter alkaline soils but the addition of acidic organic matter like peat will help. Also apply flowers of sulphur at 4 oz per sq yard on sandy soils and double this on heavy soils. Whatever the type of soil you have, and whatever its pH reading, you will also need to use fertilisers. These will either be organic or inorganic, though the wise gardener will use a combination. This way he gives back to the soil all the goodness it uses in growing the crops. Organic fertilisers contain carbon and encourage soil bacteria and thus fertility but this process is slow. Inorganic ones do not contain carbon and thus do not improve soil texture but they are full of nutrients, are quick-acting and far cheaper. All commercial fertilisers should be labelled to show their content in terms of nitrogen (N), potash (K_2O) and phosphoric acid (P_2O_5).

It is important to match your fertilisers to the needs of your garden and plants. Most will simply need a dressing of a compound fertiliser – one which supplies a combination of nitrogen, potash and phosphoric acid – before sowing, and a top dressing during the growing season. But some particular types of the so-called 'straight' fertilisers will supply particular needs. One strong in nitrogen, for instance, can be used to promote rapid leaf and shoot growth. One rich in phosphates promotes root activity and one rich in potash helps to promote heavy fruiting in a range of crops like tomatoes, beans and apples. Always remember, however, that the most important thing is to give the soil a balanced mixture of nutrients suitable for a crop. Too much of one may cancel out the effect of others.

Digging

Sad to say, no-one has yet invented a substitute for digging. The process, tiring though it may be, is crucial. It helps control the growth of weeds, improves soil texture and helps work in your manure and fertilisers. It is best done in autumn and winter since it then allows wind and rain to act on the rough clods you have turned over and break them down. However, digging when the ground is either very wet or frozen is pointless hard work and could also be bad for your soil. There are two main digging techniques.

Single digging. This is adequate for most needs, especially with loamy or sandy soils, and does not disturb the soil as much as double digging. Dig a trench across the plot removing soil to a width just greater than the blade of your spade. Retain this soil. Subsequent trenches can be dug normally throwing the earth forward into the empty trench in front of you. Dig in annual weeds which will rot down but remove and burn perennial ones. If digging in compost or manure, make sure it is all covered. When you reach the final trench fill with the retained soil from the first.

Double digging. Far more laborious and only necessary if the plot is being cultivated for the first time or has a hard sub-soil. It involves digging two spits deep. To save moving a lot of soil up and down your plot divide it in half lengthways, so that soil removed from the first trench can be placed just beyond the end of the adjacent section. Dig the first trench one spit deep and about 1.5 ft wide then use a fork to break up and remove soil for the second spit. Double digging allows roots to penetrate more deeply, improves drainage and releases more nutrients into the soil.

THE PLOT

Design. As we have explained, careful planning, even in a small garden, can give you a good supply of fruit and vegetables. But it is important to decide, when planning or re-planning your garden, just what space you want to give to fruit and vegetables and how much you will need for flowers, lawns, patio or other things.

Draw a scale version of your plot allocating the amount of space you want to give to each. In doing so, bear in mind the following advice. Vegetables should be grown in open, if possible sheltered, sites where they will get plenty of sun. They cannot be grown successfully within the rooting area of trees. Fruit should be planned carefully taking into account the needs of the climbing varieties which will require support.

Once planted, tree, bush and cane fruits will be there for a long time – as much as 50 years for tree fruits and 15 for soft fruits – so make sure you get it right. Remember, too, the height and spread of trees when they are fully grown. Few people these days have the room for a full fruit garden which is a shame, but even a small space can give a good yield. You will, of course, have to wait until your trees and canes reach maturity but salad crops can be grown between trees and bushes in the meantime. Which fruits you grow will depend on the time you

are prepared to wait and your own particular tastes, but this guide should give some useful information.

Making the best use of your plot. In order to get the best out of your plot a system of crop rotation should be followed. This is important if you are to avoid a build-up of pests and diseases. Crop rotation also allows you to control your plants nutritional needs. Here is a typical crop rotation plan based on a three-year cycle for a plot which has been divided into three sections.

Unless you are careful there will be times when your plot lies idle and, thus, unproductive. As soon as a crop is taken out make sure that another follows. This is called successional cropping. For instance, many crops like peas, broccoli and spring cabbage are harvested when the growing season is at its peak. Plan to capitalise on this with some quick growing crops like beetroot, French beans or lettuces. Clear away the remains of the old crop, fork the soil lightly to break it up, dress with a good compound fertiliser and water your drills well before sowing. Another way of making full use of your plot is to sow catch-crops in the few weeks that separate harvesting one main crop and planting another. Quick-grown salad vegetables can be raised in the intervening time.

Tools and equipment. A number of basic tools are needed

by the gardener but not nearly as many as the average garden shop or centre would have you believe. These days, tools, especially good ones, are expensive but if bought from a reputable dealer they should last you a long time. It is false economy to buy cheaply unless you are planning a short gardening career.

You will only need one spade but it must be sturdy with a blade measuring roughly 7″ by 11′. It is better to buy stainless steel because this protects against rust and slices more easily through the soil.

A four-pronged fork is invaluable for working in between rows of plants, for breaking up lumpy soil, lifting roots and other tasks.

You will need a hoe for controlling weeds between crops, making drills for sowing, drawing up soil around plants like potatoes, and other tasks. A pair of secateurs is vital for pruning and should be kept rust-free and sharp. A wheelbarrow is similarly important and, while there are many cheap ones on the market, it would be best to invest in one which has a strong barrow and a large wheel if your back muscles are not to suffer.

A rake is necessary for the fine levelling of your soil especially in seed beds, and you should make sure you choose a well-balanced one. Finally, a hose is the only satisfactory way of watering. Buy plastic. When planting you may also need a watering can with a fine and a course rose.

In addition to basic tools which can be a sizeable outlay in themselves, many gardeners will choose to invest in either a greenhouse, cold frame or some other system of environmental control designed to better aid the survival and development of young plants.

Cold frames provide control over the environment in which your hardy plants grow and develop. They increase soil temperature, allow in light, cut out weeds and pests and reduce the fluctuations in temperature which can kill off tender young plants. They can be home-made but make sure you use glass and not plastic since this conserves the heat better. The drawback with cold frames is that when it gets hot the air temperature builds up enormously and they will need to be opened up, which reduces humidity, or shaded, which reduces photosynthesis. Greenhouses are a more sophisticated and considerably more expensive investment. Metal ones are the cheapest but when buying make sure it has a sturdy frame because experience has shown that in high winds metal frames can buckle. The greenhouse helps to lengthen the gardening year. For the busy and ambitious gardener a greenhouse can be paid for over a number of years by savings in plants raised from seed and by producing vegetables at a time when they are very expensive in the shops. But if you cannot afford a greenhouse why not consider the much less expensive lean-to type, which is basically a cold-frame standing upright against the wall. Plants can also be forced into early growth by the use of

cloches. Set in a line with the ends closed to draughts they give early protection to plants allowing you to get them into the soil about two weeks earlier than normal and thus enabling you to grow more than one crop in the same season. For instance, lettuces sown in October can be cut in April giving way to dwarf tomatoes which in turn can be followed by spring cabbages. Generally speaking polythene cloches are cheapest but solid plastic ones more durable.

fruit	form	yield	time until cropping (years)	spacing
apple	bush	60-120 lb	2-4	12-18 ft
	dwarfbush	30- 50 lb	2-4	8-15 ft
	standard	100-400 lb	2-4	18-30 ft
pear	bush	40-100 lb	2-4	8-15 ft
	dwarfbush	20- 40 lb	2-4	8-15 fr
	standard	80-240 lb	2-4	18-30 fr
plum	pyramid	30- 50 lb	3	10-12 ft
cherry	morello	30-40 lb	4-5	12-18 ft
black currant	bush	10- 12 lb	2	5- 6ft
raspberry	cane	1.5 lb per foot	1	15-18 ins
strawberry		8-10 oz per foot	1	12-15 ins
gooseberry	bush	6- 8 lb	1-2	4- 5ft
red currant	bush	8- 10 lb	1-2	5 ft

Crop rotation plan

year one	year two	year three
manure	**fertiliser + lime**	**fertiliser**
onions, peas, lettuce, celery, leeks, tomatoes	brussels sprouts, cabbages, broccoli, cauliflower and other brassicas	beetroot, carrots, potatoes, parsnips and other root crops
fertiliser	**manure**	**fertiliser + lime**
beetroot, carrots, potatoes, parsnips, and other root crops	onions, peas, lettuce, celery, leeks, tomatoes	brussels sprouts, cabbages, broccoli, cauliflower and other brassicas
fertiliser + lime	**fertiliser**	**manure**
brussels sprouts, cabbages, broccoli, cauliflower and other brassicas	beetroot, carrots, potaoes, parsnips and other root crops	onions, peas, lettuce, celery, leeks, tomatoes

PROPAGATION

Propagation is simply the process by which one increases and reproduces plants. The techniques involved are no more than modern adaptations of the processes which occur in nature.

Seeds

Raising plants from seed is not only far cheaper than buying costly plants, it means you have enormous scope in what you grow because you will find much more variety in seed packets than you will at your garden shop in plant form. In addition to this, however, growing from seed is tremendously rewarding. The process requires only a little knowledge, care and patience.

All common vegetable seeds have to be tested in accordance with U.K. seed regulations so purity and viability have declared minimum percentages. This means that you are very unlikely to end up buying a bad packet of seeds. When buying you have to know that there are so called F1 varieties that have greater vigour and are more uniform in cropping than ordinary varieties. Naturally you will have to pay extra for these and you can't save seeds from home-grown plants.

Make sure when buying that you have with you a cropping plan so that you will know not only exactly what you want but also how much. As a rough guide allow one packet of seeds for a row of 30 ft. Some

seeds from crops can be saved but generally speaking it is only worth keeping larger ones. Put seeds in a dry, well-aired place for a week or so to thoroughly dry out and then store in envelopes remembering to mark the name on them. In order to germinate, a seed needs warmth, moisture and air so your soil, whether in seed trays or in the open, must be damp.

Sowing in containers. Soak the seeds in water for 12-24 hours and then sow into a container which has been filled with a suitable seed compost. Cover the seeds by lightly sieving compost over them and then label the tray. Water using a can with a fine rose or a house-plant spray, then cover with a pane of glass to keep them warm and a sheet of paper to reduce temperature fluctuations. As soon as seedlings appear remove the paper and glass and place in a well-lit spot. Water regularly but not too much. When they are ready to be pricked out, gently remove a clump and transplant individual seed-lings into the new tray or pots. Water and place in a warm spot. Once they have been pricked out they will need to be gradually prepared for survival outside. This process is called 'hardening off' and involves moving them to a cooler environment before planting outside in the open. A cold frame is best since this allows you to acclimatise the plants slowly by raising the lid for longer and longer periods until it is up day and night. At this point they are ready for planting in the open.

Sowing in the open. Be sure that the weather conditions are suited to the type of seed you plan to sow direct into the open. Clear information should be included on the packet. Sow in soil that has been well dug and manured and at a time when the soil is dry enough not to stick to your boots. Rake to a fine tilth and with a hoe make a straight drill.

Straight rows make the best use of your plot and are easier to maintain and identify especially during the early growing period. If sowing in summer the soil should be well-watered the day before sowing. Large seeds or pellets can be sown easily but be careful not to be wasteful when sowing small seed.

Cover by shuffling the soil back over the drills with your feet and then gently firm it down. If you firm down too hard then the seedlings may have trouble breaking through.

Planting vegetables. Timing is often crucial in planting out, especially with vegetables raised under glass or in a seed bed.

Wait, if you can, for mild, still weather. If the soil is dry, water it thoroughly the day before and water the plants one or two hours before moving them. Tender crops like courgettes, tomatoes and cucumbers may suffer if roots are disturbed so they are usually grown in peat pots which can go straight into the soil. If not tap plants but very gently.

Planting fruits. Before you plant, cut back any damaged roots and trim any long ones. With trees, first hold the tree over the planting site to get an idea of the spread of the roots so you can gauge the size of the hole you need to dig. If staking, place the tree about 4 ins from the stake, spread the roots and sift fine soil over them. Settle the soil between the roots and then firm it in with your feet. With cordons (single-stemmed fruit trees), plant so that the stem leans slightly to the north to give maximum light. All trees will have a knob-like projection towards the bottom which is the union between stock and scion. Make sure it is 4-5 ins above soil level so the scion does not form roots. Bushes should be planted in a similar fashion.

Trees and bushes can have roots disturbed by frost so watch for cracking of the soil. During dry spells water copiously.

Vegetative propagation

There are two main methods of multiplying plants. We have already dealt with the first – seeds – and the second is called vegetative propagation. This involves some other part of the plant that is not seed. There are four main categories: cuttings, division, layering and grafting. The latter technique is probably too complicated and ambitious for the average amateur gardener.

Cuttings. There are various forms of cuttings: stem, leaf, and root cuttings. As the names suggest, stem cuttings are taken from the stem of the plant, leaf cuttings from the leaf though usually with a piece of the stalk attached and root cuttings from a piece of the root.

Stem cuttings can be taken from young growth (soft cuttings), semi-mature growth (half-ripe) and from end-of-season cuttings (hardwood). Soft cuttings are usually taken in the spring, half-ripe in the summer and hardwood in the autumn, especially for increasing bush fruits like currants and gooseberries.

Cuttings are usually taken from just below the leaf or joint where roots most readily develop. With half-ripe and hardwood cuttings a heel (sliver of old branch) is usually taken with it. Soft-cuttings will need to be kept in a humid atmosphere.

Insert in cutting compost in a propagator, warming the soil in order to promote fast root formation in two or three weeks.

Half-ripe cuttings are a little sturdier but will still need moist, still air. Root in a propagator or a pot placed inside a polythene bag. They will take about a month to root. Hardwood cuttings should not suffer at all and can be planted outdoors if they are from hardy varieties or in a cold-frame or greenhouse if they are tender. They may, however, take several months to root. It may be necessary to increase root production and, in this case, use a rooting hormone powder.

These are usually sold with a combined fungicide which will help prevent diseases attacking the cuttings while they are rooting. With soft and half-ripe cuttings remove lower leaves to reduce demands for moisture, dip the base of the cuttings in water and then in hormone powder. Place gently in the pot or bed.

With soft-cuttings use a dibber to make the holes, while half-ripe cuttings can simply be pushed in. Hardwood cuttings can be placed in lines in trenches formed with the blade of a spade.

Once good roots have been formed, your cuttings will

start to grow again but in order to check root formation lift one or two. If they seem alright then pot on individually in a potting compost and keep in moist, still air until strong and well-established.

Division. This is usually very simple, requiring only the breaking of the plant into several pieces. Division is usually only practised on plants that produce a crown or clump of roots at, or just below, ground level. Ones that are loosely-structured can usually be pulled apart. Tougher ones can be levered apart with two forks and with very strong plants it may even be necessary to cut with a sharp knife.

Layering. This is a natural method of increasing plants which involves taking cuttings which are not separated from the plant until they have rooted. It particularly suits plants with long runners like strawberries. Most woody plants can be layered and the technique often succeeds where normal cuttings have failed. Select a flexible stem and bend it to the ground. Slit the underside at a joint to promote rooting and then bury the stem in a trench of cutting compost, keeping it down with a peg or hoop until it has rooted. Done in the spring, the layers should have formed enough roots to allow you to separate them from the parent plant and transplant in the autumn.

With climbers, it may not be convenient to take the stems down to the soil, in which case 'air-layering' is practised. After slitting and dusting in hormone powder the stems can be wrapped in wet sphagnum moss with a covering of polythene film and tied at each end to retain moisture. When roots have formed then cut, pot or plant.

Pruning

fruit	jan	feb	mar	apr	may	jun	jul	aug	sept	oct	nov	dec
apple (bush)	●	●									●	●
apple (½standard)	●	●									●	●
apple (cordon)							●	●				
blackberry										●	●	●
black currant								●	●			
cherry							●	●				
damson							●	●				
gooseberry	●	●	●							●	●	●
loganberry										●	●	●
peach								●	●			
pear (bush)	●	●									●	●
pear (½standard)	●	●									●	●
pear (cordon)							●	●				
plum			●	●								
red currant	●	●	●									

CARE DURING GROWTH

Watering

A supply of water is clearly critical in the growing process. With vegetable crops the timing can be crucial. Too much water, or too little, at any given time can be very damaging. As a rule, an inch of water will reach down 9 ins into the soil. Apply this guideline to a garden with, say, a quarter of an acre and you can see that a staggering 5,662 gallons would be needed to really reach down into the roots where it does most good.

A light sprinkling of water may dampen the soil but it won't be enough to nourish the plants. And with sandy soils, which dry out much quicker than others, watering becomes even more critical. With vegetables the really crucial time is the peak growing season when a shortage of water will impede growth and reduce crops. In order to check if they are getting enough water, dig down those 9 ins into the soil and if there is no moisture they will need a good watering. This does not, however, apply to most fruits which need water in early summer. But in late summer, when fruits begin to ripen, too much water can actually do harm.

Weeds

Weeds not only carry pests and diseases which can damage and kill your crops but they rob them of both water and light. There are basically two types of weed: annuals and perennials. Annuals complete a full life-cycle in a growing season and produce seeds which multiply the weeds. Perennials, which are less obdurate, can however survive through the winter. Among the commoner annuals are meadow grass, chickweed, nettles, speedwell and groundsel. Some of the more common perennials include bindweed, dock, thistle and couch grass.

Controlling annuals is a continual and never-ending chore.

When digging in the winter bury them at the bottom of the trench along with the compost or manure.

Perennials are easier to deal with. Cut them down during winter digging and remove all roots, if necessary doubledigging the plot. Whatever weeds you have, you will need to hoe regularly between April and July. Always try and deal with these weeds before they can get established. It's no good leaving a limp pile of weeds on the soil because, especially in wet weather, they can re-establish themselves. Weeds can also be controlled by mulching. Dry soil, black polythene, compost or peat can form a barrier between plants and any potential weed. In the case of black polythene this has the added advantage of warming up the soil and maintaining moisture. An organic mulch like peat can be dug back into the soil when it has served its original purpose and thus improves your plot.

There are also chemical weedkillers that can do an effective job for you. Usually these are only employed against annuals. Always be very careful when using them because careless spraying can do more harm than good. There are three basic types of weedkiller: one which destroys everything, one which is selective in what it kills and one which is a pre-emergence weedkiller, preventing weed seed from germinating.

Fertilisers

The three major ingredients plants need for good growth are nitrogen, potassium and phosphorus. A shortage of nitrogen shows itself rapidly in pale green leaves and slow development. Potassium, or potash as it is more commonly known, is not generally held to be beneficial in itself but is vital as a catalyst associated with food-manufacture for plants and in the process of photosynthesis. A deficiency in potash can be spotted when leaf-edges turn first yellow and then brown and appear scorched. Phosphorus is a vital protein in the plant structure and is important both for vigorous root development and for the production of flowers and seeds. Stunted growth and a purple or red leaf discolouration may be a clue to

phosphate deficiency. If a plant shows, for instance, a potash deficiency buy a brand of liquid fertiliser high in potash nutrients.

Plants also need magnesium, sulphur, manganese, iron, boron, zinc, copper, chlorine and molybdenum but these are usually found in sufficient quantity in the soil. They are known as 'trace elements' because only small quantities are required. Organic fertilisers like bone meal, which releases phosphates over two or three years, and hoof and horn, which slowly releases nitrogen, are too slow to administer to the needs of plants showing these deficiencies. An inorganic fertiliser is really the only answer. Organic fertilisers are generally used as pre-sowing dressings or top dressings only.

Pruning

The very idea of attacking a lovingly tended tree or bush with a pair of sharp secateurs is enough to inhibit many gardeners. But the process is not only a reasonably simple one it is also good for the trees and bushes and vital in producing healthy and heavy crops.

If you don't prune, the tree may grow happily for a couple of years but it will gradually produce more fruit of a poor quality and put forth less and less growth. If you overprune, however, you can produce too little fruit and too much vegetative growth. Keeping a healthy balance between growth and fruit is the secret of pruning. It also allows light and air to get at the tree or bush. To achieve all this you will need to prune at different times of the year according to the type of tree or bush and further on in this section is a pruning guide which will help you.

The harder you prune, in other words the more you cut back, the more vigorous the growth and the stiffness of the remaining branch. Summer pruning is usually done with trees and bushes that have been trained to grow up walls, fences or trellis like espaliers and cordons. But training fruit trees and bushes can slow down cropping and most are easier to control and more productive if you encourage the natural growth habits. A good rule to follow is that the more vertical a branch grows the more vigorous the growth will be, while the more horizontal it is the healthier the fruit buds it will produce. When pruning for new growth always cut cleanly with a pair of sharp secateurs. Start your cut on the opposite side to a growth bud slanting across and upwards to a point just above it. If your cut is too close to the bud you may damage it but if it is too far away the resulting stub may die or harbour disease.

PESTS AND DISEASES

The best way to avoid pests and diseases is to grow strong, healthy plants. They stand less chance of succumbing to disease and are better able to ward off the threat of pests. But even in the best-run garden damage through both pests and disease can occur. In trying to minimise this the secret is to keep a very close eye on your crops, in particular during the spring when they may be young and vulnerable. The sooner you take action the more likely it is to work.

This may involve the use of chemicals, though some people will prefer not to use these and will try to cultivate in a completely natural fashion using no pesticides or chemical fertilisers. Such methods may require certain sacrifices in the visual appeal of your crop – apples, for instance, can appear scabby – but organic gardeners will swear that the taste of fruit and vegetables grown naturally more than makes up for this. Before considering the use of chemical methods there are a number of ways of guarding against such problems. Start with good, sturdy plants and make sure you take care of them. Rotate your crops as described in our chapter on your plot. Potatoes, for instance, may well develop a build-up of eelworm if grown year after year on the same spot. In a similar way brassicas cultivated in the same position can become infected with club-root. In addition, try to create a weed-free, healthy environment for your plants. This will discourage the development of diseases. When raising your own plants from seed make sure that you use fresh seeds bought from a reputable dealer. You can save a few pence by buying cheap seed that has been in the packet a long time, but the penalties of doing this far outweigh the advantages. Probably you can use seeds from varieties that are resistant for some diseases. If saving your own seeds the same rules apply. Try to ensure quick germination when growing from seed and do not overwater.

Finally, if infection or pests appear try and remove the source of the problem rapidly. Using chemicals can often be the most effective way of destroying pests and diseases but there are other, less drastic measures.

Biological controls like the use of predators in a green house can reduce pest problems. Whitefly, for instance, can be a big problem with some green house crops. Research has shown that this can be kept down by the introduction of a few small wasps especially the Encarsia formosa.

Similarly, birds like tits can be encouraged because they prize the small moth larvae that can destroy your apple crop.

If you do have to use chemicals then there are a number of

important rules to follow;
* Do not spray indiscriminately. This may be harmful to your crops and could destroy those predators which naturally destroy pests.
* All chemicals should be locked up and kept well out of reach of children.
* Follow the manufacturers instructions to the letter and make sure you wash out thoroughly any containers used in the process. If one particular pesticide hasn't worked this may be because the pests have built up an immunity. In this case another can be tried.
* Never spray on a windy day and be very careful not to allow the spray to drift onto neighbouring crops or someone else's garden, ditches or into water courses.

The most common garden pests are aphids, whitefly, slugs and birds.

Aphids attack most bush, cane, soft fruit and vegetable crops. They also spread viral diseases. In fruits, overwintering eggs can be killed by spraying with a tar oil wash in December (not strawberries). If aphids are still present in spring a systemic insecticide should be used. For vegetables spray at the earliest possible stage with dimethoate unless the crop is to be harvested within a week in which case use derris.

Slugs and snails can destroy almost all seedlings and growing crops but can be controlled by using methiocarb pellets.

Whitefly attacks tomatoes, brassicas and other vegetables leaving a black, sooty deposit on the leaves. Control is possible with 3 or 4 sprays of pyrethroid compounds at seven-day intervals.

Birds can devastate most crops and unfortunately most bird scarers and repellant sprays are pretty ineffective. The only satisfactory way of guarding against bird attack is with proper, well-constructed, carefully erected cages or netting. The presence in your garden of a household cat will also prove an effective deterrent. The following charts indicate the method of treatment for pests and diseases among the more common fruit and vegetables. If your particular problem is not included then consult a good garden centre or shop.

An infected plant

A healthy plant

PESTS AND DISEASES

Crop	Symptoms	Causes	Non-chemical treatment	Chemical treatment
Apples	yellow mottling on leaves	red spider mite	predatory mite Phytoseiulus Persimius	DNOC in winter, wash Feb.
	sunken, discoloured patches on bark	canker	cut out, burn diseased parts	spray with dinocap before flowering or with benomyl as flowering starts
	red, yellow curled leaves, distorted fruit	aphids		dimethoate as leaves emerge
	white fungal spores	mildew	remove affected areas	spray with dinocap at pink bud stage and every 10 days until mid July
	maggoty apples	codling moth caterpillars		spray fenitrotion or malathion mid-June and three weeks later
	white fan-shaped sheets of growth beneath the bark of the roots and the trunk of the tree at ground level	honey fungus	dug tree out and burn it; sterilize the ground	
Cherries	round, brown spots on leaves	bacterial canker	remove dead wood, paint with wound treatment	bordeaux mixture in late summer
Currants (red and white)	white, powdery coat on young leaves	American gooseberry mildew	cut and burn diseased shoots in Aug./Sept.	dinocap before flowering; benomyl as flowers open
	blustered, distorted leaves	aphids		tar-oil in jan.; dimethoate in Apr.
	rotting berries, grey or brown fluff	grey mould	destroy affected fruit	spray with benomyl when flowers open and at 2 week intervals until 6 weeks
	dark brown spots on leaves	leaf spot	burn diseased leaves	benomyl before flowers open
	swollen ruds	big bud mite	burn affected shoots Jan.-March	benomyl
	coral red spots on old and dead wood	coral spot	cut out and burn the affected branches; paint the wound with a protective paint	
Currants (black)	severe reduction in crop	reversion	dug out and burn diseased bushed	
Goose berries (white)	white, powdery coat	American gooseberry mildew	burn diseased shoots in Aug.	dinocap before flowering
	dark brown spots on leaves	leaf spot	burn diseased leaves	benomyl before flowers open and at 2, 4 and 6 weeks

PESTS AND DISEASES

Crop	Symptoms	Causes	Non-chemical treatment	Chemical treatment
	defoliation in middle of bush	sawfly (caterpillar)	pick Apr.-May	derris spray
	eaten buds	bullfinches	erect nets over plants about Nov. to Apr.	
Peaches	round brown spots	bacterial canker	remove bad branches and paint wound	bordeaux mixture in mid-Aug.
	distorted leaves	peach leaf curl		bordeaux mixture Jan.-Feb. and again at leaf fall
	white, powdery fungus on shoots	powdery mildew	cut out infected shoots spring-summer	sulpher fungicide every 2 weeks
	infested young shoots	aphids		tar-oil in Dec.; malathion, dimethoate or formotion after blossoming
Pears	discoloured patches on bark	apple canker	cut and burn diseased parts and paint wounds	bordeaux mixture after harvesting and before leaf fall
	distorted fruit	boron deficiency		1 oz boray per 20 sq yards (mix with sand)
	leaves brown and withered, shoots die back	fireblight		notify ministry of agriculture
	brown or black scabs	scab	burnleaves in autumn; cut out scabby shoots on pruning	benomyl ad budburst and every 2 weeks as necessary until late june
	poor growth, wilting	aphids, caterpillars		malathion, nicotine, pirimicarb
	brown pustules in the leaves; premature leaf-fall	pear leaf blister mite	handpick and destroy infested leaves	lime-sulphur end March
Plums	curled leaves and clusters of aphids	aphids		dimethoate before and after flowering
	brown spots	bacterial canker	cut out affected wood	bordeaux mixture mid-Aug. and Sept., Oct.
	bright yellow spots on leaves	plum rust (in weak trees only)	burn fallen leaves; feed, water, mulch	thiriam
	rotting fruits	brown rot	remove and destroy affected fruits	thiophanatemethyl in mid-Aug. and Sept.
Rasp-, black-, logan-berries	purple blotches on buds	spur blight	cut out affected areas	benomyl at 2 week intervals until flowering

PESTS AND DISEASES

Crop	Symptoms	Causes	Non-chemical treatment	Chemical treatment
	purple spots on canes in June, split canes	canespot	burn affected canes	benomyl at 2 week intervals until flowering
	poor growth, yellow blotches or mottling	raspberry virus	burn all affected plants at same time; plant new canes 50 ft away	
	mottled discoloration or foliage	red spider mite (glasshouse)	predatory mite Phytoseiulus persimius	dimothoate 3 or 4 times at 7 day intervals
Straw-berries	brown patches on fruit, grey growth	grey mould	destroy affected fruit	benomyl as flowers open and at 2, 4 and 6 weeks
	large brown blotches, withered fruit	strawberry leaf blotch	burn affected leaves	dichlofluanid 2 weeks before flowers and 10-14 days after
	purple patches on leaves, grey fungus	mildew		benomyl after flowering and 2 weeks later
	shiny black beetles	strawberry beetle	trap in jar sunk to rim in soil	methiocarb pellets before strawing
	slugs			methiocarb pellets
Beans	weak plants, black fly near shoot tips	aphids	pinch out tops of broad bean plants in flower	dimethoate
	discoloration of leaves and stems	chocolate spot	sow thinly, potash at 0.5 oz per sq yard before new sowing	copper fungicide on young foliage before symptoms show
	spots on leaves with light halo effect	halo blight	no control, burn crop	
Brassi-cas	stunted plants, wilting roots	clubroot	lime in soil, rotate crops, improve drainage	dip roots at planting in benlate
	leaf spot fungi, dark brown spots	leaf spot	remove and destroy affected leaves, thin and rotate crops	benomyl
	weak plants, wilting, blush leaves	cabbage rootfly	crop rotation	diazinon before sowing or planting; trichlorphon drench on established plants
	black sooty deposit on leaves	white fly	biological control under glass with the wasp compound Encarsia formosa	3-4 sprays of pyrethroid
	yellow leaves, week plants	mealy cabbage aphid		dimethoate

PESTS AND DISEASES

Crop	Symptoms	Causes	Non-chemical treatment	Chemical treatment
Carrots	stunted growth, tunnels under roots	carrot fly	delay sowing until end of May, thin sowing	diazinon
Lettuce	greenfly	aphids		dimethoate
	yellow blotches on leaves	downy mildew	thin sowing; remove affected leaves	zineb
	weak and wilting plants	root aphids	sow resistant variety like 'Avoncrisp'	diazinon
Onions	grey mould on store crop	neck rot fungus	store only hard, well dried bulbs	
	flussy white growth at base	white rot	burn affected plants immediately	benomyl
	rotting plants, swollen tissue	eelworms	burn infected plants	
	young plants dying, older bulbs tunneld	onion fly		diazinon when planting
Peas	maggots in peas	pea moth	late-sown, early maturing varieties	fenitrothon 7-10 days after flowering
	leaf margins nibbled	pea weevil		pirimiphos-methyl dust
	brown, black or yellow insects sucking sap	pea thrips		dimethoate
Potatoes	yellow foliage and collapsed roots	blackleg	destroy affected plants	
	scabs	common scab	keep well watered, especially in dry spells	
	foliage, stems and tubers diseased	potato blight	deep planting of healthy tubers in 5 ins drills, earthed up in time	main crop sprayed only onwards with zineb or bordeaux mixture
	narrow tunnels in tubers	wireworms	plant early varieties	at planting, treat soil with diazinon

PRESERVING

Some gardeners deliberately plan for a crop surplus in order that they can eat all they need fresh and have plenty left over for preserving. There is a variety of methods suitable for home preserving.

Bottling

Set aside an afternoon free from all other chores so you can give it your full attention. You will need large, strong glass jars with lids capable of creating a vacuum seal. You will also need a thermometer, a pan deep enough for the complete immersion of your jars and some tongs for removing them.

Your fruit should be cleaned, trimmed and any brown or squashy bits removed. Bottle them in whatever form you prefer – whole, peeled, cored, quartered or sliced.

Next you will need to make the syrup in which they are to be bottled.

Use water and granulated sugar – 8 oz of sugar to 1 pt of water – melting the sugar slowly into the water over a low heat. Stir regularly and bring to the boil. Simmer for a few minutes. Fill the warmed bottles with your fruit, pour in the hot syrup to the brim and then screw on your lids. Screw tightly and then unscrew them half a turn or so in order to let the air escape (very important). Place the jars in your deep pan on a false bottom or trivet. Completely fill the pan with warm water (38 °C) so

that the jars are submerged. Bring water to simmering point (88 °C) over 30 minutes. Maintain heat for 2-40 mins according to our chart. Remove jars from pan, tighten the seals immediately and leave to cool.

Fruit	Simmering Time
Apples (solid)	20 mins
Apples (sliced)	2 mins
Apricots	10 mins
Blackberries	2 mins
Cherries	10 mins
Gooseberries (dessert)	10 mins
Gooseberries (green)	2 mins
Loganberries	2 mins
Peaches	20 mins
Pears	40 mins
Plums (whole)	20 mins
Plums (halves)	20 mins
Rhubarb	2 mins

Drying

Fruit. One of the oldest and cheapest methods of drying is to use the sun but in temperate climates one can seldom guarantee a supply of uninterrupted sun and a cloudless sky. Instead we use the sun and wind and supplement this with other forms of heat. In theory almost any fruit can be dried but for satisfactory results stick to apples, pears, plums, cherries, peaches, apricots and grapes.

Clean, wash and trim fruit into manageable slices or bits or, if you wish, leave them whole.

Apples. Use ripe apples, either eaters or cookers. Drop into

lightly salted water to stop any browning, shake and thread onto thin sticks or spread out onto trays. Place in a cool oven or airing cupboard (60 °C) for 4-6 hours.

Pears. Peel, core and quarter. Sprinkle with ascorbic acid to stop browning, spread on trays covered with cheesecloth and dry in the same way as apples.

Peaches. Peel, halve and stone. Sprinkle with ascorbic acid, spread on trays hollow side up and dry at no more than 50-65 °C. They will dry in 15 hours.

Apricots. Remove stone through a slit but do not peel. Sprinkle with ascorbic acid and dry as for peaches except at a temperature of 50 °C in an oven or airing cupboard. Up to 2 days is necessary. They are dry when no juice flows and skin remains unbroken when squeezed.

Grapes. Wash, dry in a cloth and spread on trays covered with cheesecloth. Dry in an airing cupboard or oven at a temperature rising slowly to 65 °C for about 8 hours. Cool overnight and store.

Plums. Scald whole in boiling water to split skins. Halve, stone and proceed as for pears.

Cherries. Leave stalks on and stones in. Spread on covered trays and dry at 54 °C for 6 hours.

Vegetables. Because vegetables contain less acid and little or no natural sugar they are more difficult to dry and if the process is interrupted will go mouldy. Root vegetables can be stored in peat or sand so drying is unnecessary but otherwise only onions, garlic, peppers, French and runner beans dry satisfactorily.

Onions can be dried whole or peeled. If drying whole they need to be spread out on wire mesh or something similar so that they dry evenly, and left in the sun for several days. When skins get brown and papery hang them up inside. To dry sliced, cut them into 0.5 inch thick slices, spread on trays covered with cheesecloth and dry for 8 hours in the sun. They are ready when brittle.

Garlic can be dried whole in a similar fashion to onions except their skin will get papery but not brown.

Peppers. Slice into rings removing stalk, seeds and the white fleshy part. Spread on trays and dry in a very low oven for 3 hours. Ready when brittle.

French and runner beans. Prepare in the same way as you would to cook them. Blanch in boiling water for 3 mins, them rinse in cold water. Soak up excess water in a cloth and dry on trays in a cool oven or airing cupboard until hard. Pack in airtight containers.

Freezing.
Although more expensive than bottling, drying or other methods, freezing is quicker, simpler and allows you to retain your fruit and vegetables in the form that you know them fresh.

Soft fruit, tree fruits and most vegetables can be frozen. When selecting a freezer make sure you buy one suitable for your needs. Frozen food must be packaged properly and this means either plastic bags, plastic boxes, aluminium foil or waxed containers.

Only freeze food that is fresh

and in good condition and always try to freeze as soon after picking or buying as possible.

Cool anything hot before freezing and never re-freeze without cooking first. Finally, always remember both to label and date your frozen produce so you know what it is and how long it has been there.

Vegetables. Just about all your summer vegetables can be frozen. Only salad vegetables, whose water content makes them unsuitable, are the exception. They will all, however, have to be blanched before freezing so refer to our blanching times in the full index of fruit and vegetables beginning on page 34. When blanching, plunge into a large pan of boiling water lifting out promptly and then plunging into cold water.

Drain and dry and then pack in your freezer bags ensuring that as much air as possible has been removed. Most will keep for about a year in an ordinary freezer, although you should not keep cauliflowers more than six months and mushrooms more than three months.

Blanch and freeze in quantities which you will later need. There is little point in thawing a large bag of vegetables if you

are only going to cook a few.
Fruit. There are a number of methods for freezing fruit depending on how you intend to eat them later. Fruit for pies can be frozen, sliced or pulped while other fruit may be frozen halved or even whole. Before freezing, hull, remove any stalks, peel and slice where necessary.

Pureed. Very ripe fruit when still edible can be frozen after rubbing through a sieve and sweetening with sugar. If necessary simmer before sieving.

Sugar-frozen. Suits soft berry fruits. Freeze the cleaned berries in layers of fruit and sugar in sturdy plastic containers. Allow up to 6 oz of caster sugar per lb of fruit.

Dry-frozen. Suits berry fruits. Spread dry fruit in layers on clean trays and freeze for about one hour then pack in containers.

Syrup-frozen. Suits fruits which don't have much natural juice like damsons, grapes and peaches. Pack fruit in sturdy plastic containers and pour on a syrup made up of between 1-2 lb of sugar per two pints water depending on the strength of syrup needed. Keep fruit fully immersed – not even a tip should be showing. Try a ball of crumpled grease-proof paper. Leave 0.5 inch space between fruit and lid to allow for expansion.

Poached. Some fruits, like apricots, plums and peaches, may become hard during freezing unless they are poached first. Simmer them, stoned and halved, in a syrup made up of 1 lb sugar to 1 pint water for a few minutes. Cool and pack.

81
VEGETABLES

So far we have dealt in fairly general terms with how to prepare the soil, how to sow and plant and how to care for your plants during growth. We have also told you about the various pests and diseases which can attack your crops. Now we shall deal in specific terms with the individual needs of fruits and vegetables. These fifty-three pages have full colour photographs of every plant so that you can properly identify them. We give the Latin and the English names and a general description.

Next we tell you specifically how to care for each type, when to sow and plant, what sort of soil they favour, whether they like moist or dry conditions and details of thinning and transplanting.

Included in these listings are details of how and when to harvest your crops and what sort of preserving methods, if any, suit them. We also give blanching times if freezing is an option. Many of the fruits and vegetables listed have so many varieties that we have included a more general introductory section covering the range and types involved. When using this guide it will pay the reader to think carefully about what sort of garden he has and how much he intends to cultivate it for fruit, how much for vegetables etc. Just as you can find yourself tempted to buy too many packets of seeds when visiting your seed merchant, you might find yourself tempted to grow too many plants for either your needs or your ability to give them sufficient attention.

Read the details carefully and judge for yourself whether the care and attention needed justifies the sort of crop you can expect. Decide whether you really need to grow more than one type, say, of cabbage, and whether the growing time of that apple tree is unrealistic given the length of time you intend to be in your home. Ambition can tend to override common sense when you see all the marvellous varieties that can be grown. But just remember: if you try to grow too much you may end up successfully growing little or nothing.

ALLIUM ascalonicum
Shallot

Description: A hardy bulbous vegetable with small onion-flavoured bulbs measuring one inch across.
Care: Grow in open, sunny position in fertile, well-drained soil. Work in fertiliser before planting 9 ins apart in rows 15 ins apart, in February or March. In June, aid ripening by raking soil away from the base of the bulbs.
Harvesting: In about mid-July, when foliage turns yellow, lift clumps and leave out to dry. When completely dry separate bulbs and store in boxes in a cool place.
Preserving: Pickle, in boxes or freeze (blanch: whole for 3 mins.).

ALLIUM cepa
Pickling onion

Description: These are small and quick-growing bulbs which, unlike most members of the onion family, are sown thickly in the spring and will be ready for pickling in July.
Care: Pickling onions will do best where the soil is light and even poor. Sow your seeds in March or April. They can either be scattered over the surface or sown in shallow drills which are about 8 ins apart. They like well-drained soil and will need little attention. Lift and divide each year in March.
Harvesting: They will be ripe in July.
Preserving: Pickled (of course).

ALLIUM cepa
Onion

Description: Biennial vegetable grown as an annual for its bulbs. It is winter hard. With a little care you can enjoy onions from your own vegetable garden all year round. For an early harvest small, partly developed onions, raised the previous year and known as onion sets, are planted. The most suitable variety for this is 'Stuttgarter'. For a crop to store in winter, use seed onions sown outdoors in the spring. The best known varieties are selections of 'Rijnsburger'. Also recommended are 'Noordhol-landse Strogele' and 'Blood Red'. The latter, as the name implies, is an onion with red flesh and not the usual white. It has a stronger flavour than the conventional onion.
Care: As stated above, there are two methods of growing onions: from seed or using onion sets. For seed onions the preference is for loam or light clay soil. The ground must contain a lot of calcium and a little nitrogen. For this reason it should be fertilised with an ordinary artificial fertiliser plus an extra addition of calcium. This should be done before sowing. The use of stable manure is not recommend-ed since it increases the likelihood of an attack on the vegetable by onion fly. Sow out in March or early April in furrows spaced 25 cm apart. Sow thinly. Thin out to 10 cm. In some years sowing out can take place as early as late February or early March, although this brings a greater chance of failure. Onions grown from seed are harvested in September or October.
Onions from sets are grown in two phases. In the first year small onions are raised, which are then used for planting out in the second year. By June, the first small onions are ready for harvesting.
These must be stored in a cool and dry place during the winter ready for planting out in the second year. Sometimes the storage presents problems, which is why some amateur gardeners use bought onion sets. Moisture retaining, fertile soil with humus is necessary for growing the small first year onions. When fertilising, take care not to add too much nitrogen. Sow out late March to early April in rows spaced about 25 cm apart. Do not thin out, since the whole idea is that the onions cannot grow too large. Lift the young bulbs late July and hang them to dry. Retain the leaves, which at this stage are still green, and only cut them off when they have turned yellow and dried out. Give the onions some more time to dry

thoroughly and then store them for the winter in a cool and dry place. In favourable weather they can be planted out the following February, but it is better to wait until late March. In a very wet spring it can even be as late as April before the onion sets are planted. Second year onions can be grown in all soils with a good lime content. Plant them in a vegetable bed that has been fertilised with an artificial manure. Again, do not use stable manure. Plant them in rows that are 30 cm apart with a distance between onions of 8-10 cm. Before planting out, sort the onions according to size. The larger ones will quickly provide bunches of small onions, which can be harvested early. The smaller sets are left to continue growing. Onion sets are planted by hand. Make sure that the tops are covered with soil. If you don't, then you run the risk that birds will pull them out of the ground to eat. Apart from onion fly, onions are also quickly susceptible to attack by stem worms and white rot. For this reason good rotation of crops is necessary. Never grow onions more than once in five years in the same plot.

Harvesting: Bunches of small onions, the second year onions with the leaves still green, can be harvested as early as June. Those onion sets left to grow larger can be lifted in August. This is done in dry weather. Remove the foliage and lift; they can then be stored for a couple of weeks. Seed onions, on the other hand, can be stored throughout the winter. These are harvested in September or October, by which time the leaf must be yellow for about two-thirds of its length.

The leaf should then be bent over to allow it to die off naturally. The onions are lifted and left to dry on the ground. To ensure dryness, they can then be hung up in bunches. In fact, in a very wet autumn, it is better to hang them immediately. The onions are not peeled; this only happens when they are needed for eating. So called 'cleaned onions' are less easy to keep. Make sure they are well dried to avoid attacks of mould in the winter.

Preserving: Onions must be stored in a cool place. The best temperature is -1 to 1°C. Store them in boxes covered with plastic in a shed or garage, and check them regularly.

ALLIUM porrum
Leek

Description: A hardy biennial vegetable grown as an annual and prized for its ability to survive the hardest of winters. Its thick, white stem is composed of tight, succulent layers of leaf bases which have a mild onion flavour and which are best blanched before harvesting. There are numerous varieties but these can be generally divided into three groups : early, mid-season and late maturing. If grown as exhibition vegetables then it is best to grow the early-maturing since most shows are held between August and November.

Care: Leeks should thrive in ordinary, well-drained soil which has been deeply dug and manured. A top dressing of fish manure two or three weeks before planting-out the seedlings is adviseable. Soil must be well-dug so they can be deeply planted and then earthed up for blanching. Germination is slow and seeds will need a soil temperature of at least 7°C. For early crops sow in a seed tray in late January to early February. Prick out into trays when leaves have straightened, spacing them 2 ins apart. Maintain temperature of at least 13°C in greenhouse or other suitable spot. Harden off in cold frame during March. Plant out in late April. For main crop leeks sow outside in March to April and transplant during late May or June. Sow thinly in drills 0.5 in deep and in rows 6 ins apart.

For June sowings, transplant in July and crops will be produced the following spring. Plants should generally be planted out when pencil thin and 6-8 ins high. Plant on the flat or in deep trenches and blanch by progressively drawing up the soil around the plants during the growing season. Water only in very dry conditions. To prevent soil getting into the plant centres during earthing-up, cardboard or paper collars may be tied around them. Leeks are generally free from most pests and diseases but they can be attacked by onion fly maggots which infest the roots causing wilting and collapse. Treat soil with diazinon when sowing.

Harvesting: To extend your harvesting period you can lift from the time they are about 0.75 inch thick. Ease out of ground with a fork and continue lifting until clear of the soil. They will keep during winter.

Preserving: Freeze (blanch: 2 mins.).

APIUM graveolens var. dulce
Self blanching celery

Description: Like other forms of celery this is a
hardy biennial but has the advantage, for some
gardeners, in that it does not require blanching.
Varieties include 'American Green', 'Golden Self-
Blanching' (white) and 'Latham Self-Blanching'.
Care: Sow seeds as for normal trench-grown
varieties but then plant out your seedlings on the flat
in soil well-dug with manure the previous April.
Plant out in May in a square 11 ins apart each way.
Do not require earthing-up and should be ready from
August to October.
Harvesting: Before frosts begin.
Preserving: Bottle or frozen (blanch: 3 mins.)

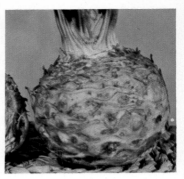

APIUM graveolens var. rapaceum
Celeriac

Description: A hardy biennial grown as an annual
for its thick roots which are used as a winter
vegetable. Resembles celery but has swollen root
similar to turnip.
Care: Fertile, well-manured, well-drained soil. Sow
seeds thinly in March in seed compost and germinate in greenhouse. Prick out and harden-off before
planting. Outdoors sow thinly in April in sunny
sheltered seed bed. Thin. Plant seedlings 12-15 ins
apart and water well.
Harvesting: Lift roots from September, blanching
in November if leaves are wanted.
Preserving: In boxes of sand or soil in cool shed.

APIUM graveolens var. secalinum
Celery

Description: A hardy biennial vegetable grown as
an annual for its crisp, tartly-flavoured stalks.
Care: Open sunny spot in well-drained, well-
manured soil. Sow seeds late March in pots at temp
13-16°C, prick out into trays 2 ins apart. Harden-off
and plant out late May or June. Sow outdoors under
cloches. In May or early June transplant seedlings to
final spot. Tie stems loosely just below leaves and
draw up soil to level halfway up set. Earth-up
periodically. Soil must not fall between stems.
Harvesting: Heads blanched 8 weeks after first
earthing.
Preserving: Bottle, freeze (blanch: 3 mins.).

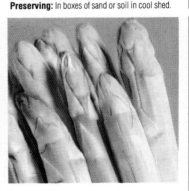

ASPARAGUS officinalis
Asparagus

Description: Hardy, perennial vegetable needing
great care and patience to grow well.
Care: Open, sheltered position, rich, well-drained,
manured soil. Grow from plants one or two years old.
Plant early April in trenches which are 3 ft apart and 8
ins deep. Put plants 18 ins apart and slowly draw up
soil around them until by December bed is level. Hoe
lightly for two years, keep watered, cutting ferns in
October. Dress each spring with fertiliser.
Harvesting: One year crowns in third year; two year
crowns in second year. Cut sparingly.
Preserving: Bottle, freeze (blanch: 3 mins.).

ATRIPLEX hortensis
Orache

Description: Sometimes known as 'Mountain Spinach' there are three forms of this annual: green, white or red.
Care: Sow seeds thinly in soil which is well-drained, but moisture retentive, from the end of March to end of July in rows 18 ins apart. Thin early to 15 ins. Water when dry and hoe to keep down weeds.
Harvesting: May to October. Gather some leaves from each plant rather than stripping one. Young leaves for salads, older cooked like spinach.
Preserving: Not suited.

BARBAREA praecox
American cress

Description: Despite its name it is almost unknown in America. An excellent substitute for watercress this perennial needs no water for growing and is easier to manage. Its tender young shoots are splendid in salads and soups.
Care: First sowings in late March in damp, shady spot. Prepare seed bed with organic matter, rake to fine tilth and sow in drills 9 ins apart and 0.5 in deep. Keep soil moist, do not thin.
Harvesting: Pick from late June onwards.
Preserving: Not suited.

BETA vulgaris
Beetroot

Description: A biennial root vegetable grown as an annual. Tender, dark red flesh used for cooking and pickling or with salads and soups.
Care: Light, fertile soil which has been well-dug, fertilised and broken to a fine tilth. Successional sowings of seeds from late March to early July. Sow main crop in late May. Sow thinly in 0.75 in drills in rows 12 ins apart thinning to 5 ins or 8 ins for long-rooted varieties.
Harvesting: Pull up when large enough. Leave main crop until required if protected with straw.
Preserving: Boxes of sand or earth. Freeze small and cooked. Bottle or pickle.

BETA vulgaris var. cicla
Spinach beet

Description: A perennial beet which makes a fine substitute for true spinach. It produces nutritious green leaves but no beet-root. Leaves are larger, more fleshy and easier to cook than spinach.
Care: Make one sowing in April and another in late August if a year-round supply is needed. Sow in rich soil in drills 1 in deep and 15 ins apart. Thin to 8 ins. Keep roots moist when it is dry.
Harvesting: Continue to pick young leaves even when not using them to avoid loss of production and quality.
Preserving: Not suited.

BRASSICA
Cabbage

Introduction

Probably more time and effort is spent in producing vegetables from the brassica family – cauliflowers, cabbages, broccoli, Brussels sprouts, kale etc. – than any other. It is because they are so well-suited to the climate of Northern Europe that brassicas figure prominently in the gardens of most growers. In the following section we deal with the particular growing requirements of a variety of brassicas but there are a number of general rules which apply to the cultivation of them all.

Firstly, for practical reasons, it is best to raise your brassicas first in a seedbed. This will save you occupying your main brassica bed for 5-7 weeks with tender seedlings when you could be employing the space for something more productive. Nurturing the young seedlings in a special seedbed allows you to give them proper care and attention while freeing valuable growing space. Once the initial period of growing has elapsed they can then be transplanted. All brassicas should be dealt with in this fashion with the possible exception of some varieties of Chinese cabbage and kale.

Brassicas like a fertile soil but should not be grown on the same site in your garden more than one year in three. Rotating the growing site has a number of advantages, the main one of which is to help stop any build up of club-root which distorts the roots and is a serious threat to the growth of all brassica plants. This disease is especially prevalent in acid soils so if this applies to your garden the addition of ground chalk or limestone at 14 oz per square yard followed by periodic smaller dressings should help to raise the pH level to a more satisfactory 6.5 to 7.5. If a plot has suffered from an attack of club-root then no brassicas should be grown there again for at least seven years. There are a number of vegetables, however, which are resistent to club-root and can be safely grown on the site instead.

Rotating the growing site for brassicas also has other advantages. For instance, if you have grown peas and beans the year before, moving your brassicas to that site will enable them to take advantage of the nitrogen levels left in the soil on which they thrive. Brassicas like firm soil which has preferably been double-dug the previous winter and dressed with well-rotted manure or compost at a rate of one per square yard. Recent experiments have shown that considerable increases in cropping can be gained by planting in deeply-prepared soil. All brassicas thirst for water and the deeper their roots are able to freely penetrate the better they can search out water.

Prepare the seedbed in an open, sunny and fairly sheltered spot which ideally has been manured for a previous crop. Before you sow top dress with a general fertiliser at around 2 oz per square yard and rake into a fine tilth. Water copiously before sowing and prepare shallow drills about 0.75 in deep and 6 ins apart. To stop any threat of a damping-off disease dust the seeds with thiram before sowing. Germination will take between 7 and 12 days. Thin to about 2 ins apart, water and weed. Most young brassicas will be ready to transplant in about 6 or 7 weeks when they have developed 3 or 4 leaves and have grown to a height of 4-6 ins. Water thoroughly the day before transplanting.

Before re-planting dip the roots of the seedlings in calomel paste to control any attack of cabbage root fly or club-root. Water until they become established and it is particularly hot protect the young seedlings with a covering of newspaper during the day. About three days after planting the seedlings place diazinon in the soil around the base of each plant to give them further protection against attacks of cabbage root fly.

Most brassicas are easy to grow and will be good croppers. This does not apply, however, to the cauliflower – surely the most difficult of all the family to cultivate. Producing that tight, white head is something which has frustrated many a gardener and any minor setback like a spell of very dry weather or a check in growth for some reason, is likely to lead to unsatisfactory results.

We have already mentioned club-root but most brassicas are also subject to the risk of attack from aphids, cabbage root fly, cabbage whitefly, caterpillars and flea beetles. Methods for treating these pests and diseases are dealt with fully in a special chapter.

BRASSICA cernua
Chinese cabbage

Description: A quick-growing cabbage which is similar to a cos lettuce and can be used both as a green and a salad vegetable.
Care: Sow seeds in June direct into the soil where the plants are to grow. Favours light soil but needs to be well watered in dry spells. Sow in rows 15 ins apart and thin to 12 ins apart. Sow successionally for a regular supply and it will be ready through late summer and early autumn.
Harvesting: Cut in a similar fashion to cabbage.
Preserving: Not suited.

BRASSICA juncea
Chinese mustard

Description: Sometimes known as mustard greens these are common in the United States and can be found in tins and jars in Europe. It is hardy, resistant to hot, dry weather and grows when other green stuff is in short supply.
Care: Sow seed from April to August in rows 15 ins apart. Thin seedlings to 6 ins. Rich, moist soil. It will grow rapidly and can crop within 8 weeks giving succulent leaves not unlike chinese cabbage. Enrich soil with nitrogenous fertiliser especially if poor.
Harvesting: Will run to seed so cut entire plant rather than just picking leaves.
Preserving: Not suited.

BRASSICA napus
Swede

Description: A hardy biennial grown as an annual winter vegetable largely for its fleshy, swollen yellow roots.
Care: All fertile soils except acid ones. Grow in soil manured for previous crop and dig bed thoroughly, raking in fish manure. Sow seeds in mid-May, or a little later in southern areas, in 1 in deep drills, 18 ins apart. Thin to 12 ins.
Harvesting: Roots can be lifted from autumn until spring and can be left in ground during the winter.
Preserving: Store in clumps ensuring a supply when ground is frozen. Not for freezing.

BRASSICA napus
Foliage of swede

The roots of swedes, if lifted in mid-winter and trimmed, can be used to produce a very nutritious partly blanched growth that can be eaten like any green vegetable, boiled, braised or steamed. Lift the roots in the middle of the winter and after trimming pack in boxes of peat or soil and place in a cool, dark place like a garage. They will sprout, producing a part-blanched growth. Just pick and cook when needed. They do not suit any form of preserving.

BRASSICA oleracea var. acephale laciniata
Kale

Description: Hardy biennial plant grown as an
annual for green winter vegetables. Developed from
wild cabbage and valued because they crop in
January to April when little else does.
Care: Well-drained, medium soil manured for a
previous crop. Dress with fertiliser. Sow seeds
outdoors in seed bed in mid-May, thin and transplant to final plot in July planting with 24 ins each
way.
Harvesting: Leaves are ready for picking any time
from Christmas onwards. Pick from centre of plant.
Preserving: Eat fresh only.

BRASSICA oleracea var. botrytis cymosa
Broccoli

Description: Hardy vegetable which comes in two
types, curding and sprouting. The curding, also
known as winter cauliflower, is similar to the
cauliflower except in texture and colour. The
sprouting variety has shoots bearing heads of white
or purple unopened flowers.
Care: Sow seeds in outdoor seed beds from March
to May in 0.5 in deep drills, 12 ins apart. Thin and
transplant to main bed allowing 24 ins each way.
Water well, dress lightly with nitro-chalk.
Harvesting: Curding variety as for cauliflower.
Sprouting, cut 12 ins long shoots.
Preserving: Freeze shoots (blanch: 3-4 mins.).

BRASSICA oleracea var. botrytis cauliflora
Cauliflower

Description: A half hardy biennial plant, grown as
an annual vegetable for its thick clusters of florets
which grow at the centres of large, thick leaves.
Different varieties mature successively during the
year and they can generally be divided into three
groups : summer, autumn and winter cauliflowers.
The cauliflower, though one of the favourite
brassicas for eating, is perhaps one of the most
difficult to grow because it makes great demands in
what it requires of soil, moisture and food.
Care: If good crops are to be grown a deeply-dug,
fertile soil rich in humus is essential. Plenty of
manure added to the soil during digging will help to
retain moisture. Cauliflowers are less hardy than
many other brassicas and so the site should be
reasonably sheltered. Even overwintering varieties
may not escape damage in severe conditions. Before
planting rake in a good general fertiliser at about 3 oz
per square yard.
Early cauliflowers can be grown by sowing seed in
January in a temperature of 13°C for crops in June
and July. Prick out into cold frames when large
enough to handle, harden off and plant out in March.
Autumn cauliflowers are grown in seedbeds during
April and May for crops in September to December.
Transplant in late June to growing site. Space at 22-
30 ins according to size of variety. Winter cauliflowers are not so demanding as others but are unlikely
to withstand long periods of frost. They mature
during December and late May or June, depending
on varieties. Seed is sown thinly in seedbeds from
mid-April to mid-May and in June or July transplanted to growing site which has been dressed with
general fertiliser about two weeks before. Allow 30
ins between plants for winter cauliflowers. As curds
begin to develop protect them against cold weather
by snapping one or two leaves over them for
protection.
Cauliflowers are subject to attack by aphids, cabbage
root fly, club-root and damping off. See Pests and
Diseases for treatment.
Harvesting: Cut heads when firm. If they mature
together don't let them break up, pull and hang
upside down in a cool shed.
Preserving: Pickle, bottle or freeze (blanch: 3
mins.).

BRASSICA oleracea var. bullata gemmifera
Brussels sprouts

Description: Hardy vegetable rich in vitamin C and thought to be descendant of wild cabbage. Crops autumn and winter if early and late varieties grown.
Care: First sowings of early varieties in mid-March in sheltered seed bed. Sow 0.5 in deep in drills 9 ins apart. Thin to 2 ins. Sow maincrop varieties in April. Grow in fertile soil with adequate lime content. Ideally soil should have been well-manured for previous crop.
Harvesting: Pick when small like nuts and ideally after a frost. Pick from bottom up.
Preserving: Bottled, frozen (blanch: 1.5 mins.).

BRASSICA oleracea var. bullata sabauda
Savoy cabbage

Description: A round-headed, flat-topped cabbage with thick, wrinkled leaves. It is very hardy and will give a crop through winter to May.
Care: Sow seeds in a prepared bed in the same way as for other previously mentioned cabbages. If sown in April you should have a crop from September to December. If sown in May it will crop January to March. A July sowing crops the following April and May. Transplant seedlings to growing site six weeks after sowing, planting them 18 ins apart and with 2 ft between rows.
Harvesting and preserving: As for other cabbages.

BRASSICA oleracea var. capitata alba
Spring cabbage

Description: The original wild cabbage has long been outstripped by a range of varieties, all of which have been highly developed to suit a particular purpose. The small-growing spring cabbages are generally grown for cutting when they are still young giving an early supply of cabbage and treating those who grow them to a crisp, fresh-tasting treat at a time when other garden vegetables may be scarce. Also known as coleworts, or collards, spring greens are cut at any time between November and April. Of the many varieties 'First Early Market 218' and 'Wintergreen' are among the best suited. When autumn sowing to produce spring crops it is vital that the gardener chooses varieties which have been specially bred for the purpose. Those that have not will be susceptible to bolting and this can be an enormous waste of time, effort and money. Among the earliest to mature is a variety called 'Harbinger' which has a small, dark-green head. Maturing slightly later than 'Harbinger' are varieties 'Wheeler's Imperial', 'April' and 'Durham Elf'. If you are looking for a larger head than other early-maturing varieties, ones which will suit include 'Flower of Spring' and 'Early Offenham'.
Care: All cabbages do well in ordinary, well-drained garden soil, but for spring cabbages the preference is for a slightly lighter soil. Prepare the bed in early winter by digging thoroughly and enriching with a good bucketfull of well-rotted compost or manure for every square yard. If the soil is lime rich you won't need to add carbonate of lime – otherwise rake in 4 oz per square yard in the spring.
Sow seeds in the last week of July where the plants are to grow. Try and use soil vacated by some early-maturing vegetable crop. Hoe and sow thinly. You will later need to thin seedlings to about 5 ins apart. When harvesting, cut the cabbages young and crisp. Don't wait too long for them to develop since they are meant to be eaten smallish, though winter maturing cabbages can be left in the bed for a longer period than others.
Pests which can attack cabbages include aphids, birds, maggots of the cabbage root fly and flea-beatles. Diseases include club-root, damping off, wire stem, leaf spot and grey mould.
Harvesting: From November to April.
Preserving: Not suited.

BRASSICA oleracea
White beefheart cabbage

Description: This is an early sowing variety of cabbage which is then harvested in the summer and early autumn. When sowing, however, remember that it matures at about the same time as many other vegetables so do not sow more than you will be able to eat.
Care: Sow March and April in a plot well prepared in late February. Sowing in frames in February for planting out in April, gives even earlier crops. Sow thinly, 1 in deep and 6 ins apart. Water drills beforehand.
Harvesting: From late July until autumn.
Preserving: Pickled.

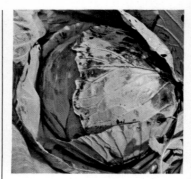

BRASSICA oleracea var. capitata rubra
Red cabbage

Description: Biennial vegetable cultivated as an annual and, in this variety, often grown for pickling. Solid heads, crisp leaves. Makes good autumn and winter crop.
Care: Sunny open site in well-drained, alkaline soil. Dig in manure and spread lime unless soil is chalky. Sow in seed beds as for capitata. Apply a general fertiliser at 2 oz per square yard. Leave seeds in seedbed through autumn and winter protecting with cloches. Transplant in April 2 ft apart.
Harvesting: Cut when firm and fleshy.
Preserving: Freeze young and shredded (blanch: 1.5 min.)

BRASSICA oleracea var. gongylodes
Kohl-rabi

Description: A quick-maturing biennial vegetable grown as an annual. Can withstand frosts and store for several weeks. Swollen stem similar to turnip is eaten as a vegetable.
Care: Fertile, well-drained soil. Sow seeds in drills 0.5 in deep in the growing site in rows 15 ins apart. Thin to 9 ins and keep well-watered. The crop will mature rapidly – in only 10-12 weeks from sowing. For constant supply sow at four-week intervals from March.
Harvesting: Pull plants when bulbous stems are the size of tennis balls.
Preserving: Freeze small roots (blanch: 3 mins.).

BRASSICA pabularia
Turnip tops

Description: In addition to being a splendidly nourishing winter vegetable the turnip can also provide the gardener with rich, nutritious leaves which can be eaten as a winter vegetable. The young shoots, incidentally, can also be eaten, blanched and used as a substitute for sea-kale.
Care: Sow outdoors in September. No thinning will be necessary. Cut the foliage when it is about 8 ins high which should be around eight to ten weeks after sowing. A good variety for this use is 'Greentop White'.
Harvesting: Cut tops with a knife when ready.
Preserving: Not suited.

BRASSICA rapa
Turnip

Description: Half-hardy biennial grown as an annual vegetable. White, slightly mustard-flavoured roots are eaten. Harvest throughout most of the year.
Care: Light fertile soil in sunny spot but not in freshly manured ground. Sow in February under cloches or in frames but keep frost-free. Outdoor sowings in sheltered spot in March. Sow again in April and May for summer supply and in July and August for winter crops. Sow in 0.5 in drills 15 ins apart, thin to 3 ins then to 6 ins and keep watered.
Harvesting: Pick regularly when tennis ball sized.
Preserving: Store in shed. Freeze summer crop (blanch: 2 mins.)

CAPSICUM annuum
Red pepper

Description: Perennial shrub usually grown as an annual. It bears red conical fruit used in sauces, curries and pickles. For vinegar use the ripe fruits. Often grown for ornamental purposes.
Care: Can be grown outside but does better under glass. Sow seeds in March in warmth, plant outside after frosts in sunny, sheltered position in soil prepared with well-rotted manure. Before re-planting rake in a general fertiliser. During flowering period syringe leaves daily. When fruits appear liquid feed until ripe.
Harvesting: Pick when red during September.
Preserving: Pickled or dried.

CAPSICUM annuum
Peppers

This whole family of sweet peppers has been ignored by many gardeners because they assume they are difficult to grow. Others believe that because they are called peppers they are hot. But properly grown they are magnificent and will not give you nearly as much trouble as you suppose. Plants can be grown in exactly the same way as aubergines, sown in seed trays and grown in sunny, sheltered positions outdoors or under cloches and cold frames in shallow trenches. Green peppers are really only the red and yellow sort before they start to turn colour. Chilli peppers are a form of capsicum which is related to the green pepper and is grown in the same fashion. For successful crops it is advisable to keep them under glass.

Even when grown out of doors, in a hot summer, you should be able to produce as many as three peppers from each plant and if grown under glass then you can expect to produce perhaps twice as many as this. For most people, between four and six outdoor and two or three indoor plants will probably be sufficient. 'Canape', an F1 hybrid is a variety which does well out of doors and under glass and matures early. 'New Ace' is another early maturing variety which is high-yielding and it is best grown in a greenhouse. In warm summers 'Worldbeater' is a good outdoor, heavy cropper.

Caterpillars are the biggest problem when growing peppers but they may also be liable to attack by grey mould. With caterpillars either pick them off by hand or treat with fenitrothion or trichlorphon. Grey mould is likely to appear in overcrowded, stagnant conditions and attack the stems, leaves and fruit which then rot rapidly. To avoid attack sow thinly, provide good ventilation when under glass and remove all dead or decaying material. Fumigate with tecnazene smokes if growing under glass. The peppers will be ready, green, in August or September and for yellow or red peppers simply leave them to turn colour.

CICHORIUM endivia
Endive

Description: A half hardy annual grown as a salad plant since the 16th century for its pale, green, slightly bitter curled leaves. It has never achieved the popularity it perhaps deserves because of its bitter taste and the problems of blanching. It does, however, make an excellent alternative to lettuce in salads especially in late autumn and early winter. Two main types of endive are grown – the curly variety which is sown in June and July to crop in September to November, and the hardier variety which is not sown until August and which will provide a splendid winter salad vegetable well into the winter. The first variety is usually known as Staghorn while the latter is commonly called Batavian. Recommended varieties are for early sowing 'Moss Curled', for late summer 'Exquisite Curled' and for autumn and winter use 'Batavian Broad-leaved'.

Care: Endives like light, well-drained soils but will grow in heavy soil if plenty of straw and manure is dug into it. Nine or ten plants can be grown in one 10 ft row and two such rows, one with early the other with late endives, should be sufficient for most families.

Sow the seeds thinly in 0.5 in drills 15 ins apart in the growing site. Thin the seedlings as they grow until they are 12-15 ins apart. Water the bed about once a week and keep it free of weeds. For a continuous supply make the first sowing in April and further sowings at four week intervals until mid-August. Sow late maturing varieties in a sheltered sunny position or under glass. Plants will generally be ready for blanching about three months after sowing. Gather the leaves together when dry and tie to keep out the light from all but outside leaves. Another method would be to cover with boxes or pots. Blanching will take up to ten days in summer and up to three weeks in winter.

Harvesting: Cut as for lettuces but only when needed since they don't keep.
Preserving: Not suited.

CICHORIUM endivia var. crispum
Curly endive

Description: A variety of endive, prized for its curly leaves, which provides salad vegetable from September to November – earlier than the hardier wavy-leaved type.
Care: Thrives in light, well-drained soil. Sow in June or July 0.5 in deep in drills 15 ins apart, in growing site. Water thoroughly, weed and thin to 12-15 ins. To save seeds, sow three or four at 12-15 ins intervals and remove the weakest after germination. Blanch to create the crisp white-heart as described earlier.
Harvesting: Cut from the base with sharp knife.
Preserving: Not suited.

CICHORIUM intybus
Green chicory

Description: Variety 'Sugar Loaf' like previous varieties is a hardy perennial grown as an annual and can be forced but can also be grown as a salad or green vegetable picked in summer and cooked or eaten raw.
Care: As for chicory.
Harvesting: Pick in summer, cutting from the base of the plant.
Preserving: Not suited.

CICHORIUM intybus
Chicory

Description: A hardy perennial grown as an annual for its hearted head of leaves.
Care: Grown outdoors, then forced and blanched inside to produce the head. Sow seeds in open, May or June, in drills 0.25 in deep and 18 ins apart. Thin to 9 ins, weed and water. In October or November cut off 1 in above roots, lift and trim roots to about 8 ins. Store in cool, frost-free place or in trench below a layer of soil, until needed.
Harvesting: Force 4 or 5 at a time in pot of soil covered with another pot. Given warmth chicory will grow 6 ins in a month.
Preserving: Not suited.

CLAYTONIA perfoliata
Winter purslane

Description: A succulent plant ideal for growing as a winter salad vegetable at a time when most familiar salad vegetables refuse to appear.
Care: Sow in July in any ordinary soil and continue sowing, if successional crops wanted, until August. The winter purslane will survive several degrees of frost but the leaf quality, growth and chances of survival are improved if it is protected either by bracken or with cloches.
Harvesting: Through autumn, winter and spring.
Preserving: Not suited.

CRAMBE maritima
Seakale

Description: A hardy herbaceous perennial grown for its leaf-shoots which are blanched to produce tender, asparagus-like vegetable.
Care: Can be raised from seed or thongs. Plant during winter or March 2 ft apart in 2 ft rows with tips 2 ins below soil level. Water, feed and mulch (in May). Remove flowering stems to promote shoot-growth. Sow seed 0.5 in deep in March or April, thin to 6 ins and leave plants to grow for a year. Re-plant 2 ft apart etc.
Harvesting: Force roots in pots of soil (7 weeks). Cut shoots when 6 ins tall. Eat fresh.
Preserving: Not suited.

CUCUMIS melo
Melon

Description: Tender annual grown for large, edible sweet fruits. Grow in greenhouse or under cloches.
Care: Warm, moist, well-manured soil. Sow indoors in artificial heat in mid-April, in 3 ins pots, 0.5 in deep, one seed per pot. Germinate, pot-on and plant-out under cloches mid-May on, 3 ft apart. Pinch-out growing point when 4-5 new leaves appear, then later select 4 strong shoots and pinch-out the rest. Train two in each direction and allow one melon to form on each. Remove any other fruit.
Harvesting: Cut only when completely ripe.
Preserving: Bottled or frozen.

CUCUMIS sativus
Ridge cucumber, gherkin

Description: Half-hardy annual trailing plant grown
as a salad vegetable whose smaller-growing types
are also pickled.
Care: Sow 2-3 seeds 0.5 in deep in late April in peat
pots. Place in airing cupboard or near heater and
when seedlings appear, retain strongest and harden
off during May. Plant out 2 ft apart in well-dug,
manured soil at end of May-early June. Pinch-out
growing tip at 6-7 leaf stage. May be necessary to
pollinate. Feed regularly and keep fruit off soil with
board or glass.
Harvesting: Before maximum growth.
Preserving: Pickled, bottled.

CUCUMIS sativus
Frame cucumber

Description: Also known as glass or greenhouse
cucumbers, these varieties produce best crops under
glass at minimum 21°C.
Care: Sow seeds in late February or early March
singly in 3 in pots of seed compost. Will germinate in
the greenhouse in 4-5 days. Place in maximum light,
and when at 3 true-leaf stage pot on into 5 ins pots,
with lower stem covered. Fix a vertical stake by each
plant and rig horizontal wires. When plants have
reached roof, pinch-out leading shoots.
Harvesting: As for ridge cucumbers.
Preserving: As for ridge cucumbers.

CUCURBITA maxima
Pumpkin, squashe

Description: Bushy, trailing, half-hardy annuals
native to tropical countries.
Care: Thrive in full sun and rich, well-drained soil.
Dig holes 15 ins square, fill with well-rotted
compost. Sow one or two seeds in 3 ins pots in late
April/early May and germinate at 18-21°C. Harden-
off in cold frame and plant in growing site late May/
early June, 3 ft apart. Pinch-out growing point at 5-
leaf stage. Water thoroughly if dry.
Harvesting: Cut small varieties as they mature.
Leave large ones until late autumn.
Preserving: Pickled, bottled, stored frost-free.

CUCURBITA pepo
Marrow, courgette

Description: Half-hardy bushy or trailing annual
now mostly grown small as courgettes rather than
large as marrows.
Care: Sunny spot, deep, rich soil. Plant direct or
sow from seed indoors, 1 in deep in peat pots. Place
in cold frame or on window sill. Remove weaker
plants and plant out in peat pots at end of May. Bush
marrows and courgettes 2 ft apart, trailing marrows
3-4 ft apart. May need to be pollinated.
Harvesting: Vigorous croppers so cut young and
fresh. Can leave marrow late on stalk until Oct.
Preserving: Pickled, bottled, frozen (blanch: 1-3
mins.).

CYNARA cardunculus
Cardoon

Description: Handsome plant with great purple flowers and silvery leaves. Resembles the globe artichoke. Underrated as a vegetable.
Care: Rich, retentive but good-draining soil. Grown in trenches like celery. Dig trench 1 ft wide in early April leaving soil on each side. Fork in well-rotted manure. Sow seeds late April in threes, 20 ins apart, 0.5 in deep. Use cloche for first month, thin weaker seedlings. Water generously and feed. In September blanch.
Harvesting: Tie leaves wrap in black polythene. Earth-up and dig up in about one month.
Preserving: Store in polythene.

CYNARA scolymus
Globe artichoke

Description: Perennial plant grown as a summer vegetable for its flower scales.
Care: Open, sunny spot, rich, well-drained soil. Buy young plants or suckers in April, plant and in May mulch with manure or compost. In first year remove buds to encourage growth in subsequent seasons. In 2nd and 3rd years allow only 4-6 stems per plant. Leave flower on main stem at the end of one or two lateral shoots. Nip-off extra buds. In November cut main stems almost to ground, draw up soil and cover with straw.
Harvesting: Cut heads in June/July.
Preserving: Freeze (blanch: 5-7 mins.).

DAUCUS carota
Carrot

Description: Carrots can be roughly divided into three types. Bunched carrots are rather small and crisp and are harvested early in the season. Worth consideration among the varieties of bunched carrots are 'Amsterdam forcing' and 'Nantes'. Summer carrots, as the name implies, are harvested later in the season. Winter carrots are only ready in October. Winter varieties recommended for cultivation are 'St. Valery' and 'New Red Intermediate'. Both form a strong top foliage with large carrots which, unlike summer carrots, can be kept for quite a long time. Carrot is a native, biennial and winter hard vegetable, grown as an annual for its orange, nourishing roots.
Care: Bunched carrots can be sown out as early as February in a sheltered spot. Protect the seedlings with plastic. The usual time for sowing bunched carrots is from March to June. Sow not too thickly in 1 in deep furrows that are 6 ins apart. Bunched carrots should not be thinned out. Summer carrots are sown in 0.5 in deep furrows, 8 ins apart. They are first thinned out to 2 ins and later to 4 ins. Sow summer carrots from mid-April to July, although some can also be sown out under glass in March. Bunched and summer carrots are harvested 3-4 months after sowing.
Winter carrots are sown out from April to mid-July in 1 in deep furrows, 1 ft apart. Thin out to 6 ins. Carrots can suffer from carrot fly and greedy mice. Mice will eat the bunched and summer carrots if they are left too long in the ground. 'Nantes', in particular, seems to be a favourite snack for these creatures. To prevent attack by carrot fly do not use stable manure either for the actual carrot plot or the ground surrounding it. When thinning out, make sure that soil is pushed into the spaces left around the plants.
Harvesting: Bunched and summer carrots are lifted from the ground by their foliage. You may need to use a rake or fork for leverage. Winter carrots are harvested from October. The foliage is cut off to 1 in above the ground and the whole bunch lifted.
Preserving: Bunched and summer carrots are most delicious when eaten fresh. They also freeze well (blanch for 4 minutes), but they lose their flavour if stored in boxes of sand. Unlike winter carrots, which store well.

FOENICULUM dulce
Florence fennel

Description: Hardy perennial herb grown as an annual for its fat stem base used as a vegetable.
Care: Requires more attention than common fennel and needs sunny spot, well-drained soil manured the previous season and top-dressed shortly before sowing. Sow seeds thinly in 0.5 in drill in April, thinning to 12 ins. Water well and when stem bases begin to swell draw earth around them as you would for potatoes.
Harvesting: Collect stem bases for cooking or salads in late summer/early autumn. Use leaves for flavouring.
Preserving: Freeze (blanch: 3 mins.).

GLYCINE max
Soya bean

Description: Difficult to grow in this climate. Variety 'Fiskeby V' improves chance. Twice as rich in protein as any other vegetable.
Care: Warm site is vital. In autumn or winter dig in well-rotted manure, top dress before sowing. Sow in May in 2 ins drills, 3 ins apart with 12 ins between rows. Cover with netting. Seedlings appear in three weeks. Can be sown indoors in pots and then transplanted at beginning of June. Will grow to 30 ins so support with sticks.
Harvesting: Fresh in August or September. Dried on the plant for storing.
Preserving: In tins or bags when shelled.

HELIANTHUS tuberosus
Jerusalem artichoke

Description: Hardy perennial grown for its potato-like tubers used as winter vegetables.
Care: Warm, well-drained spot. Plant tubers 18 ins apart and 5 ins deep in furrows during February or March. Allow 3 ft between rows. Leave ridge of soil 2 ins high above tops, add dressing of fertiliser and hoe into surface. Draw up soil another 1 in when stalks are 6 ins high repeating process fortnightly until ridge is 6 ins high. Then stake or care plants, run wires between and tie up with soft string.
Harvesting: Lift at end of October.
Preserving: Not suited.

IPOMOEA batatas
Sweet potato

Description: Sometimes, but incorrectly, called a yam, this is a creeping perennial plant of the Morning Glory family which is grown for its fleshy underground roots which are cooked and eaten like the yam.
Care: Very difficult to grow in temperate areas unless in hot-house conditions. It needs a long, warm growing season and lots of rain. It is commercially-grown in southern states of the USA. Needs sandy, loamy soil. Plant 1.5 ft apart in rows 3.5 ft apart.
Harvesting: When fresh-cut surface dries quickly.
Preserving: Not suited.

LACTUCA
Lettuce

Introduction

Description: Though popular with both the Greeks and the Romans, lettuces probably have an even longer history dating back thousands more years to when they were grown in the Far East.

The soft, round-headed lettuce is still the most commonly grown and sold in most parts though why this should be is quite mystifying. The increasingly familiar crisp-hearted summer lettuces of the Cos variety are far better value and have a better taste. Also for economy the non-hearted leaf lettuce is a very useful variety. Recent research has shown that using certain varieties like the 'Lobjoits Cos' and sowing seed in drills 5 ins apart and at the rate of about 15 to each 12 inch run, the plants will form crisp upright leaves which can be cut when about 4-5 ins high and be eaten like any other lettuce. The sheer economy comes from the fact that the plant re-sprouts to give more leaves and takes only between 40-60 days depending on the season to produce a far heavier crop than normal forms of lettuce which take up to twice as long.

Although traditionally associated with the summer the lettuce is a salad vegetable that can really be enjoyed in all seasons if the use of cloches, greenhouse or cold frames is employed.

There are so many different varieties of lettuce that it would be difficult to mention them all but they generally fall into one of three categories.

Cabbage lettuces which include the so-called butterheads and the crispheads, will usually grow in poorish soils and are more likely to survive than the other varieties.

Cos lettuce, though usually associated with only one type, is a category that covers a wide variety of the more upright growing lettuces with crisp leaves. They grow best in richer soils and some of the modern varieties have been developed so that they do not need tying to produce the compact heart that makes them so popular.

Leaf lettuce is a type of non-hearting lettuce which produces lots and lots of curly leaves but no true heart. If picked sparingly they will continue to grow and produce more leaves at a later stage.

Summer varieties are sown in March to July, thinned when large enough to handle, transplanted in March to April and harvested between June and October. Overwintering varieties are sown in September, thinned in October when large enough to handle, have a second thinning in March and can be harvested the following April or May. Forced varieties are sown in August, thinned when large enough to handle, transplanted under glass in September and harvested between November and December.

Lettuces are also grown under glass in which case they will be sown in October to January, thinned first when they are about 0.5 an in high, thinned again in late-February and harvested between March and May.

Lettuces can be attacked by anything from birds to slugs and from leaf aphids to grey mould. Birds, slugs and cutworm can be relatively succesfully controlled. With birds you will need strong netting or a vegetable cage. Slugs are treated with methiocarb pellets and cutworm, the soil-dwelling caterpillars that feed on the roots, can be treated with diazinon before sowing or planting. Leaf aphids are usually controlled with a systemic aphicide like dimethoate or by applying derris as the plants reach maturity. Some varieties will be resistant to lettuce root aphids buf if not apply diazinon in the summer. Grey mould can develop in cold and damp weather in which case immediately destroy the plants and as a precaution spray others with benomyl. All lettuce viruses can spread rapidly and will show up as a sort of veined effect in the leaves. Burn the plants that have been affected and remove any weeds that could still be harbouring the virus.

LACTUCA sativa var. capitata
Cabbage lettuce

Description: Half hardy annual grown as a salad plant in a number of varieties. There are two main types – cabbage and cos.
Care: Cabbage lettuces can be divided into smooth-leaved and curled leaved varieties. Sow seeds March to late-July in drills 0.25 in deep and 12 ins apart. Thin to 3 ins and again according to variety. Do not transplant outdoor lettuces after end of April. Water well and hoe.
Harvesting: Start cutting as soon as first hearts form. Cut with knife or pull whole plant.
Preserving: Not suited.

LACTUCA sativa var. capitata
Iceberg lettuce

Description: 'Iceberg' is a variety of crisphead lettuce from the cabbage lettuce group and is grown like other varieties of cabbage lettuce.
Care: Sow seeds in March to late-July in drills 0.25 in deep and 12 ins apart. Thin to 3 ins and again according to variety. If being grown outdoors do not transplant until after the end of April. Water well and hoe.
Harvesting: Start cutting as soon as the first hearts begin to swell. Cut with a knife or pull the wole plant.
Preserving: Not suited.

LACTUCA sativa
Celtuce

Description: An unusual vegetable which comes from China and which is easy to grow and deserves to be far more popular since it has a dual purpose. The leaves are high in vitamins and can be used as lettuce while the heart or crisp centre stem can be eaten raw in salads and cooked in a fashion similar to celery – thus its name celtuce.
Care: Sow from the end of April covering seeds with 0.5 in of fine soil and leaving 1 ft between rows. Sow sparingly and often and thin to 10 ins.
Harvesting: When hearts begin to swell.
Preserving: Not suited.

LACTUCA sativa var. longifolia
Leaf lettuce

Description: A variety of lettuce which is non-hearting and produces instead lots of curled leaves. The leaves can be picked a few at a time and the plant will continue to grow producing more leaves for picking later. This can be done with one or two varieties of Cos lettuce (leaf lettuce variety 'Salad Bowl').
Care: As for other varieties of lettuce.
Harvesting: If you have grown several plants then ensure that you pick only a few leaves from each, thus allowing them time to grow again and produce more leaves.

LACTUCA sativa var. romana
Cos lettuce

Description: Cos lettuces are usually oblong and have much crisper, sweeter leaves. They withstand drought better but may take longer to grow and some varieties may need assistance to produce tight crisp centres.
Care: As for cabbage lettuces except that if they do not form a compact heart slip rubber band over leaves or tie them with a soft string.
Harvesting: As for cabbage lettuce.
Preserving: Not suited.

LENS ensculenta
Lentil

Description: A staple vegetable in many countries. Rich in vitamins, minerals and protein.
Care: Wash seeds well, soak over night in lukewarm water. Rinse thoroughly and place in a jam-jar. Cover the opening with a square of muslin or nylon (old stockings will do) and hold in place with an elastic band. Put jar in bowl open end slightly down to aid drainage and place in dark part of airing cupboard. Rinse 2-3 times a day until sprouts grow.
Harvesting: After 3-4 days when sprouts are 1 in long.
Preserving: Cooked and dried.

LEPIDIUM sativum
Cress

Description: Annual usually grown together with mustard (Sinapsis alba).
Care: A 1 oz packet of mustard and a 0.25 oz packet of cress will fill four seed pans or containers measuring 6 ins by 4 ins. Place layer of cottonwool or flannel in seed tray. Sow cress first then mustard 3 days later. Spread thickly and press down, sprinkle with luke-warm water, cover with paper. In winter place in airing rupboard – a temperature of 10-16°C is needed. Uncover when 1.5 ins high.
Harvesting: Cut 11-14 days after sowing when 2 ins long.
Preserving: Not suited.

NASTURTIUM officinalis
Watercress

Description: A hardy, aquatic perennial native to Europe and commercially grown in shallow tanks of water. Small, rounded leaves grown on branching stems. Tiny white flowers followed by long, curved seed pods.
Care: Grows best in rich sandy soil. Sow in seed boxes in early summer. Plant out 6 ins apart. Can also be propagated by cuttings taken in spring or early autumn.
Harvesting: Pick when plants are established. The more the tops are picked, the more the new supplies grow.
Preserving: Not suited.

PASTINACA sativa
Parsnip

Description: Hardy biennial root grown as an annual for long-tapering, yellowish roots which are harvested when fresh vegetables are scarce.
Care: Does best in rich, light soil and sunny position. Sow seeds in March in 0.5 in drills 15 ins apart in soil which has been fertilised. Thin when 1 in high and continue thinning until 6-9 ins apart. Hoe regularly to keep weeds down.
Harvesting: The following winter. Frosts improve the flavour. Lift roots gently.
Preserving: In soil until need.

PETROSELINUM crispum var. tuberosum
Hamburg parsley

Description: Sometimes known as turnip-rooted parsley, this is a dual-purpose vegetable the roots of which can be used like parsnips or carrots and the tops of which can be used as parsley.
Care: Grown as a root vegetable in deeply-dug soil. Sow from March onwards in drills 0.5 in deep and 15 ins apart. Thin to 8 ins. Keep weed free and well-watered.
Harvesting: Roots from early October. The foliage remains abundant during the winter.
Preserving: The roots are hardy and can be lifted as needed or pulled up and stored in boxes of moist sand in a cool, airy place.

PHASEOLUS coccineus
Runner bean

Description: Tender perennial climbing plant grown as annual.
Care: Crop better if sown in deep, well-manured soil in a sunny spot which is reasonably sheltered. Sow in seed compost mid-April or outdoors mid-May. Harden-off indoor plants and plant out at end of May. Grow plants up canes in two rows 18 ins apart with 12 ins between supports which are sunk at an angle so they cross at halfway mark. Frequent watering is needed and when they reach top of pole pinch-out to encourage side-shoots.
Harvesting: Pick when young and tender.
Preserving: Salted, and frozen (blanch: 2 mins.).

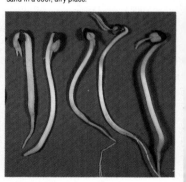

PHASEOLUS mungo
Mung bean, taugé

Description: Also known as the Chinese bean-sprout, the mung bean is one of a number of types of sprouting bean which contain a wealth of vitamins, minerals and proteins and which can be eaten shortly after germination.
Care: As for lentils, except they can also be grown in a tray.
Harvesting: Pick the crisp, white shoots when they are 2-3 ins long which should be after 4-5 days.
Preserving: Not suited.

PHASEOLUS vulgaris
French dwarf bean

Description: An annual, normally grown for its edible pods which mature from July to October. The pods are pale green, narrow and grow up to 5 ins long. Dwarf varieties save staking. Varieties grown from the French dwarf bean or kidney bean include beans which are left to dry, either in or out of their pods, and stored for eating when needed. Very convenient for winter eating, this group of dried beans has yet to make much impact in Northern Europe while it is very common in Southern Europe and in most Mediterranean coockery. Such varieties are the haricot bean and the flageolet bean, which are eaten in a variety of soups, stews and other meals. The family of beans als includes a whole range of beans which can be sprouted from seeds in jars and which mature and become ready for eating in as little as five days.

Care: The kidney bean needs light, well-drained soil and a sunny spot. The soil has to be well-dry manured in the autumn. Sow in succession to pick from late June to October. Sow 2 ins deep in rows 18 ins apart. Set in pairs 9 ins apart removing the weaker ones if both germinate. Raise early plants in seed trays in mid-April. Harden-off and plant out end of May. Support climbing varieties when 4 ins high. The haricot and flageolet are grown in the same way as the green french bean, but only the dried seeds are eaten. The flageolet is usually harvested while the beans in the pod are soft and green. Haricots, on the other hand, are left to ripen on the plant and are normally not picked until the seeds have ripened to a white or ligth brown colour depending on the variety. A recommended variety of haricot is 'Comtesse de Chambord' which produces copious amounts of small, white-seeded pods. A recommended variety of flageolet is 'Chevrier Vert'. For early crops sow seeds under cloches in mid-March and keep covered until the end of May. Non-climbing forms should be self-supporting but in sites where they are exposed it may well be necessary to stake them, and for climbing varieties cane or pea sticks will be needed. With late sowings put cloches over them in October to ensure cropping into November.

Seeds may be eaten by slugs, millipedes or the maggots of the been seed fly. With both young and established plants the aphids and especially the bean aphid will infest the terminal shoots. Capsid buys may be found feeding on young plants leaving the leaves damaged and causing blindness of the buds. Finally, in dry weather, glasshouse red spider mites may attack the leaves leaving them bronzed and withered. Among the diseases which will have to be watched out for when growing beans are foot and root rot which can be caused by a variety of funghi. The roots will blacken and die, stem bases discolour and decay, and the foliage turn yellow and wither. Grey mould can attack the pods in wet weather and if the soil is badly-drained. A variety of virus diseases can cause stunting of your plants leaving pods distorted and mottled, causing a similar effect on the leaves.

A good way of supplementing your supply of vegetables in the winter, and creating a greater variety, is to sprout seeds. This is unquestionably the most productive method of vegetable growing since the time taken from sowing to harvesting can often be as little as four or five days. What is more, the process requires no garden space, takes little time and produces an end result which is both highly nutritious in vitamins and minerals and also more exciting than many other winter vegetables. The process is quite simple and all you need is a suitable jar. Rinse in ordinary strainer and remove any which are off-colour. Soak overnight in cold water to help speed up the process. Next morning put into the strainer and run fresh cold water through them. Put them moist but drained into a deep jar in a layer no more than 0.75 inch deep. To produce the whitened sprouts, cover with a lid, plate or some moisture-retaining material, both to prevent drying out and to keep them in the dark. In cold weather they will need to be put in the airing cupboard but in summer this may not be necessary. Most seeds will sprout at temperatures of 13-21 °C. Rinse the seeds each morning and night, tipping them into the strainer and running fresh cold water through them. Put back in the jar or container and repeat the process until the shoots are the required lenght.

Harvesting: Kidney beans can be harvested from June to October Pick regularly to increase the crop. The haricot bean is harvested in September or October. Choose a dry day, pull up whole plant and hang in a dry, airy place. When pods feel crisp, shell and spread out on trays to dry thoroughly. The flageolet bean is harvested when the beans in the pods are still green and soft and then dried on trays.

Preserving: The kidney been has to be bottled or frozen (blanch 2-3 mins.). The haricot and the flageolet bean have to be dried in jars.

PISUM sativum
Green pea

Description: The green pea is a hardy, climbing annual which was once only a summer vegetable. Nowadays, because of the variety of peas available to the gardener, a careful choice can produce crops from early May to October. Generally-speaking the round-seeded types are the hardiest and can be sown to survive the winter while the wrinkle-seeded varieties are much less hardy and should not be sown until the spring. It should be pointed out, however, that while the round-seeded varieties will stretch your crops they are not generally as sweet and tasty as the wrinkle seeded ones.

For early varieties, which will be ready to be picked in May and June, try 'Feltham First' or 'Meteor'. Both are dwarf varieties which reach a height of no more than around 18 ins and can therefore be easily covered with cloches when the weather gets severe. There is a taller-growing early variety – the 'Improved Pilot' which reaches 3.5 ft. For picking in June there are a number of varieties available. Try 'Hurst Green Shaft' or 'Onward' both of which are good-croppers, generally reliable and which grow to around 2.5 ft. For main crops select wrinkle-seeded varieties since these have a higher content and therefore a sweeter flavour. For picking in July and August, these include 'Rentpayer' and 'Lord Chancellor'. The former grows to about 2 ft while 'Lord Chancellor' will reach about 4 ft. Late-crop varieties, which will be ready for picking from September onwards, will usually be the small-growing, wrinkle-seeded pea. Try quick maturing ones like 'Kelvedon Wonder' and 'Pioneer' since they are less prone to suffer from mildew. Another good variety is 'Miracle', aptly named for its ability to withstand shortages of water – something most varieties of peas hate. Bear in mind, when making your selection, that taller growing plants can produce anything up to three times as many peas as the dwarf varieties.

Care: All peas should be grown in well-drained, rich and fertile soils and if yours doesn't meet these criteria then you will need to do something about it if you are going to produce good crops. Dig in a 2 in layer of manure or well-rotted compost in the winter. This will improve the fertility of your soil. It will also help drainage because any waterlogging will rot the seeds. If your soil is poor then another additive you will need is a good application of a nitrogen compound fertilizer at the rate of around 2 oz per square yard. Apply just before sowing. Peas can either be scattered in a flat bottomed-drill about 10 ins across or sown into a V-shaped drill. Research has shown that the best crops are produced when the peas are sown in lines of three drills which are 5 ins apart and with an 18 ins gap between each group of drills. Make the drill 2 ins deep and space the peas 5 ins apart. If you are sowing into a flat-bottomed drill then it, too, should be 2 ins deep. After sowing, gently rake the soil back into the drill and then tamp it down firmly with the back of the rake. Don't waste the space between the rows, catch crops can easily be grown. Once sown, make sure that your pea crops are protected.

As soon as the seedlings are showing through you should give the rows a thorough hoe to cut down any weeds. Each plant will need the support of a stick at the side. Insert these gently and angle them outward to form a V – this will encourage open growth and light and air will be better able to penetrate especially once the peas have grown into bushy plants. They will need plenty of watering during spells and in the summer you can improve the retention of moisture and keep down the weeds by mulching the rows with peat, leaf-mould or even lawn cutting.

Peas are prone to attack from a number of pests. They include aphids, which infest young shoots and leaves and can seriously impede growth, millipedes and mice. Diseases which attack peas include damping-off, downy mildew, foot rot, grey mould, manganese deficiency and powdery mildew.

Harvesting: Pick peas as soon as you can. Do not leave them to get fat and dry on the pod because they don't taste good and they will simply reduce further cropping. Once a row has finished cropping cut down the growth and put on the compost heap, but leave in the roots. These should enrich the soil with nitrogen.

Preserving: Frozen (blanch: 2 mins.).

PISUM sativum
Sugar pea, mange tout

Description: Hardy climbing annual similar to previous varieties of peas but grown for broad, fleshy, stringless young pods that are harvested and cooked whole.
Care: As for other peas.
Harvesting: Pick when still young, crisp and juicy. Should be eaten almost immediately either fresh in salads or cooked – briefly. Steaming or stir-frying are most likely to retain the delightful fresh, sugary taste.

PISUM sativum
Marrowfat pea

Description: The marrowfat pea is the wrinkle-seeded variety which is grown as a main and late-crop pea. It is distinguished from the round-headed pea not only because of its size and shape but also because it has more sugar content – and thus a much sweeter taste. Varieties include the 'Kelvedon Wonder', (up to 2 ft), 'Hurst's Green Shaft' (2.5 ft), 'Onward' (2.5 ft), 'Dwarf Greensleeves' (3.5 ft), 'Lord Chancellor' (4 ft), 'Pioneer' (2 ft), 'Rentpayer' (2 ft) and 'Progress No. 9' (2 ft).
Care: Wrinkle-seeded varieties are not hardy and can only be sown from spring onwards. Otherwise proceed as in the green pea.

PORTULACA sativa
Purslane

Description: Grown for centuries in Europe this useful plant is an annual with succulent foliage. The young leaves can be cooked or used raw as a salad vegetable or herb.
Care: It thrives in light soil and likes a sunny spot. To ensure succession sow seeds in small batches from April onwards. Sow in rows 9 ins apart and thin seedlings to 6 ins. The seedlings can be transplanted but they should never be allowed to go short of water.
Harvesting: Pick when leaves are fully-formed.
Preserving: Dried.

RAPHANUS sativus var. niger
Black radish

Description: A hardy biennial grown, like the radish, for its crisp fiery roots which are eaten fresh with salads and in soups. The black-skinned varieties like 'Black Spanish Long' are notable for being large-rooted winter varieties.
Care: These varieties generally like fertile, well-drained soil and are sown from June to August on drills 9 ins apart. Thin to 6 ins.
Harvesting: Leave roots in the ground if you wish and pull when needed.
Preserving: In boxes of sand in cool place.

RAPHANUS sativus var. radicula
Radish

Description: A hardy biennial grown as an annual for its crisp, fiery roots. Among the quickest-maturing of all vegetables it makes an ideal catch crop.
Care: First sowing in cold frame January to February in 0.25 in drills 6 ins apart. From March on sow outside. Frequent sowings will ensure continuous crop. Do not sow thickly – 0.5-1 in is ideal; keep soil moist.
Harvesting: Pull as and when needed but they get woody if left too long in ground. Winter radishes, sown from June to August, lifted in late October.
Preserving: Store winter radishes in boxes of sand.

RAPHANUS sativus
Bavarian radish

Description: An unusual form of radish but one which has a number of uses which grows large enough to be able to cut and shape for special salad arrangements. Its roots grow to the size of turnips when properly cultivated. The decorative seed pod makes a sandwich filling when green.
Care: Easy to grow in rich, fertile soil which has been deeply dug. Roots may be small and stringy in thin soil lacking in phosphates. Sow like other forms of radish.
Harvesting: Lift roots gently with a fork. Top growth may reach 3 ft.
Preserving: Not suited.

RHEUM rhaponticum
Rhubarb

Description: A hardy perennial grown for its edible red stems.
Care: Rhubarb roots penetrate deeply so give them a bed which has been well-worked with manure. Plant in March, October or November. Dig hole big enough to take the woody rootstock leaving new shoots just above ground. Tread soil in and water. Cut off flowering spikes at once. In July dress with fertiliser. After three years select clumps for forcing. Force indoors in December in peat after exposing to frost, or outdoors in Feb. under a bucket.
Harvesting: Pull stems as needed.
Preserving: Bottled, frozen.

SCORZONERA hispanica
Scorzonera

Description: Hardy perennial winter vegetable grown for its delicately-flavoured black-skinned roots.
Care: Fertile, well-drained soil in sunny spot. Ground manured for previous crops suits best. Dig trench previous winter to break up soil. Sow seeds in April/May in 0.5 in drills 15 ins apart. Thin to 8-12 ins. Hoe regularly and water well when dry.
Harvesting: Lift roots in October as needed. Can be left in soil throughout winter.
Preserving: In boxes of sand or earth.

SOLANUM lycopersicum
Tomato

Description: Generally grown in a greenhouse or indoors, tomatoes come in a profusion of varieties most of which are long-stemmed and crop over a sustained period. There are bushy varieties with short joints that do not need staking. Fruits can be red, orange or yellow; large medium or small; and grooved, plum-shaped, pear-shaped or globular. For early sowings in a heated greenhouse select one of the F1 hybrids like 'Kingley Cross'. Main crop varieties include 'Grenadier'. For sowings in an unheated greenhouse try the very popular, heavy-cropping 'Moneymaker', or for better flavour and texture 'Ailsa Craig' or 'Alicante'. For sowings out of doors the heavy-cropper but less tasteful 'Moneymaker' can again be grown, or try quick-maturing varieties like 'Histon Early'.

Tomatoes can be grown direct into your greenhouse soil but after a while will tend to build up a variety of pests and diseases so it is better to grow them in pots of compost or growing bags, which give you complete isolation from the greenhouse soil.

Care: The process of planting is largely the same whether for plants grown indoors or outdoors. The ideal time is when the flowers on the first truss are opening. Make holes with a trowel and plant them 18 ins apart each way with the top of each root ball level with the soil surface and water well.

In greenhouses watering and feeding is critical and will require a good deal of attention, while outdoors the soil will provide nutrients and water that greenhouse plants cannot expect. This rule especially applies with plants raised in totally isolated systems like grow bags which contain few nutrients and which can retain only small amounts of moisture. Bear this in mind all the time since only relatively short periods without watering or feeding can impair growth and cropping. Watering moderately and often is the only way since too much water in, say, a grow bag can be even worse. In such systems the plants may need three or four waterings in a very hot day. Add a good liquid feed to the water.

Growing in the greenhouse: Tomatoes are best raised from seeds though it can be more convenient simply to buy plants from the local garden centre.

Sow seeds 0.75 in apart in boxes of compost and cover with glass or polythene. Germinate at 16°C and as soon as the young seedlings appear remove the glass and place in the light. When seed leaves have opened pot on into 3.5 ins pots. Harden off after six weeks if they are to be grown outdoors. Greenhouse tomatoes are usually liquid fed.

Growing outdoors: Outdoor tomatoes may be planted any time from early June onwards if the climate is mild. Use frames or cloches to protect young plants and to help ripen fruit at the end of the season. In early June, before planting, add about 4 oz of tomato fertiliser per square yard to the soil. Plant with 18 ins all round and water well. Stake with bamboo canes and tie the stems loosely to them immediately after planting. If side-shoots develop remove them immediately (except on bush varieties) since they will hinder production. In all long-stemmed varieties stop the plant two leaves beyond the fourth truss as soon as the fruits begin to swell by pinching out the growing points. To ripen – in September – cut the strings and place plants on straw. Cover with cloches and continue to water without wetting the fruit.

Pollination: Generally speaking, if you have followed the basic rules, there should be little problem in getting your tomato fruit to set. There are, however, methods which can encourage setting-vibrating the bamboo care or string, tapping the flower trusses or spraying the plants with water to disperse pollen. Tomatoes can be attacked by a wide variety of pests and diseases. Leaf mould shows itself as yellow blotches on the top side of leaves or a purple/brown mould underneath. Try adding a mulch to the soil to improve texture. Grey Mould affects stems and leaves making them rot. They become covered with grey growth. It develops in overcrowded or stagnant conditions. Sow seeds more thinly, ventilate and rake decloran into soil before sowing. Damping-off is caused when seedlings are overcrowded. Sow thinly in sterilized compost. Water with zineb. Aphids cause damage themselves and carry viruses. Check for their presence regularly. Spray with derris of dimezoate. Derris if harvesting within a week. Other problems include glasshouse whitefly, potato cyst eelworm, wireworm, blossom end rot, blotchy ripening, greenback, magnesium deficiency, scald and tomato blight.

SOLANUM tuberosum
Potato

Description: The most widely grown vegetable in almost all temperate zones, this tuberous-rooted perennial is grown as an annual for its edible tubers which are one of the most versatile vegetables the gardener can grow. For millions of people the potato provides the staple source of starch. It does, however, require a good deal of space if a year's supply is to be grown. Potatoes fall into three groups according to the time of their maturing – first early, second early and main crop. The varieties will differ considerable depending on local conditions and it would be advisable to consult local opinion on what will do well.

Here, however, is a general guide to some varieties. Among first early types are 'Sutton's Foremost' and 'Home Guard'. Second early varieties include the waxy 'Craig's Royal' and the floury 'Ben Lomond'. Main crop potatoes include the heavy-cropping waxy potato 'Majestic' and the floury 'Arran Banner'. Propagation of the potato is from specially-grown tubers or 'seed potatoes' which have been saved from the previous season. You can save the tubers from your own home-grown crops but it is probably not advisable because if they become diseased your whole crop could suffer. Seed potatoes grown in 'virus free' conditions reasonably cheap and a more reliable source.

Care: Potatoes will grow in almost any soil but the ideal conditions are deep, well-dug and well-manured soil capable of holding moisture in dry conditions but which will drain well when wet. Dig in manure or compost in the autumn and then in the spring fork the ground over and rake in a general fertiliser and diazinon to protect your crop against the main threats to potatoes – wireworm and cutworm. The deeper dug the plot the better you will be able to establish your tubers and the better you can earth-up during the growing period.

Plants can be raised from small tubers bought in January and started in trays in the light until they start sprouting. Keep just two sprouts on each tuber when planting and rub off the rest. Plant them 4-5 ins deep. Early and second early varieties will need to be 12 ins apart in rows 24 ins apart while main crops should be 15 ins apart in rows 2.5 ft apart. In most areas early and second early varieties can be planted in March covering young shoots with straw to protect from late frosts. Main crop varieties can be planted in late April/early May. When shoots are about 6 ins tall begin drawing up the soil around them forming 6 ins high ridges each side. Earth-up again. After four weeks and once more after another three weeks. Always remember that seed tubers should be planted with the buds or 'eyes' upwards.

Early crop potatoes should be watered at the rate of about 3-4 gallons per square yard every two weeks in order that you can maximise your yield. It has been found that if they are watered when the small developing tubers are about the size of a marble, approximately 0.5 in in diameter and not before, they will mature earlier. Main crop potatoes will need about 4 gallons per square yard at the flowering stage. This should increase the yield significantly and in addition reduce the danger of scab.

The process of 'chitting' potatoes helps them to begin growing quickly when planted and is especially useful in early crops which only have a short growing period. To do this, place a single layer of your tubers with the 'rose' end upwards in boxes in a light, airy place. Do this in early February and by the planting time in late March you should have sturdy shoots about 0.75 – 1 in long. If you live in an area where planting has to be done a little later than normal it will probably be worthwile 'chitting' second early or main crop potatoes as well.

Very early potatoes can be grown out of season in a greenhouse or in a cold frame by planting sprouted tubers during January or February. Cover the glass with straw mats or sacking during frosts. You can also plant 2-3 chitted tubers in a large box or pot of potting compost and keep them in a slightly heated greenhouse at a temperature of 4-7°C.

Harvesting: Early potatoes should be ready about three months after planting – in around June or July. They will be ready when the flowers are fully open. Lift with a fork as you need them. Second early and main crops should be ready from August onwards. Leave the tubers on the top of the soil for 2-3 hours to dry or, if wet, in a garage or cool dry place. Lift all tubers whether you eat them or not so that no disease is left.

Preserving: Keep only the good ones and store in boxes covered with black polythene. Only freeze small earlies or chipped (blanch: 3 mins.). Chipped potatoes will need to be par-fried for 3 mins. before freezing.

SOLANUM melongena
Aubergine

Description: Tender annual plant grown in tropics. Best grown here in greenhouse. Smooth, ovoid fruits cooked in Mediterranean dishes.

Care: Sow seeds in compost in February. Propagate at 18°C. Prick out singly into 3 in pots, grow on at 16°C. Transfer to 7 in pots when 4-6 ins tall. Pinch-out tops when 9 ins high to encourage them to bush. Allow up to 3 fruits on each of 3 or 4 lateral branches. Water copiously and feed weekly.

Harvesting: Ripe when blackish/purple. July to Oct.

Preserving: Freeze (blanch: 4 mins.).

STACHYS affinis var. tubifera
Chinese artichoke

Description: Though similar in appearance to the Jerusalem artichoke this is not an artichoke. It comes from a family of plants more commonly grown for their attractive flowers. It has a flavour much like the true artichoke.

Care: Well cultivated, light soil and a sunny spot. If the soil is poor then work in manure or compost before planting in March or April. Place tubers 4 ins deep and 9 ins apart in rows 18 ins apart. In dry weather water to promote growth.

Harvesting: From November onwards. Dig up as needed.

Preserving: In cool, dark place.

SPINACIA oleracea
Spinach

Description: A group of annual vegetables grown for their edible leaves which are either cooked or eaten raw in salads and which are highly-nutritious. Spinach is hardy, quick-growing and an ideal catch crop grown between rows of cabbages, leek, peas or beans. If sown successively the summer and winter varieties can give the gardener a supply all year round. Summer varieties include the popular 'Long Standing Round' while winter crops include the hardy 'Green Market' and the bolt-resistant 'Sigma-leaf'.

Care: Summer varieties should be grown in deeply-dug, rich and moist soil which has been manured and top-dressed with fish manure. Grow in part-shade and a cool spot to avoid plants running to seed.

The first outdoor sowing should be made in early March with successional sowings following, if you want continuous crops, in three-weekly intervals until early July. The seeds should be sown thinly in 1 inch drills placed about 15 ins apart. Thin when large enough to handle, first to 6 ins and later to 1 ft. Summer sowing should be ready to be picked between May and October. When picking select leaves from a number of plants rather than stripping one bare at a time.

Winter spinach should be grown in soil prepared in the same fashion as for summer spinach and, again, successional sowings should be made if you want a regular supply. Start sowing in mid-July and up to late September. Thin seedlings first to 3 ins and later to 6 ins. Growth will be much less rapid. Protect the plants from around November onwards by placing cloches over them or thick layers of dry straw between the rows. It should be ready for picking from mid-October onwards. Once again, do not strip a plant of leaves, instead take ripe leaves from a number of plants. This way you should be able to maintain growth. If the plants are properly thinned and watered then the main threat to spinach, downy mildew, should be deterred. If it should strike then spray the plants with zineb or copper fungicide.

Harvesting: Summer spinach should be ready in 8-10 weeks. Winter spinach will take longer – about 12 weeks.

Pick young outside leaves gently. Don't tear. This will encourage continued growth and cropping.

Preserving: Best fresh. Freeze (blanch: 2 mins.).

TARAXACUM officinale
Dandelion

Description: Once the vegetable gardens of all
great houses grew dandelions for blanching like
chicory or for leaves, roots and flowers added to
salads.
Care: Prefers rich soil and protection in winter and
is propagated by division. Should grow in sufficient
profusion to provide wild crops for those seeking it.
Harvesting: Best in spring before plant comes into
full flower. Pick leaves when young and pale green.
Blanch a plant or two in winter for the spring.
Preserving: Not suited.

TETRAGONIA expansa
New Zealand spinach

Description: A native of Australasia this is a
branching, mat-forming variety that survives drought
and will grow in poor soils. Will not, however,
survive frost.
Care: As for other spinach except that it remains in
the ground much longer so cannot be grown as a
catch crop. Prefers rich, well-manured soil.
Harvesting: As for spinach.
Preserving: As for spinach.

TETRAGONOLOBUS purpureus
Asparagus pea

Description: A lesser-known, half-hardy annual
which is grown for its edible seed pods which, as the
name implies, have an asparagus-like taste. The
plant forms a bush about 1 ft high and small
brownish-red flowers are followed by cylindrical
seed pods with four wavy wing-like flanges.
Care: Sow seed in April in in deep, 6 ins apart and in
row 3.5 ft apart. Support plants with stakes.
Harvesting: Gather the pods young and fresh when
they are no more than 1.5 ins long. Cook whole.
Preserving: Eat fresh.

TRAGOPOGON porrifolius
Salsify

Description: A biennial plant often known as the
'oyster vegetable' because of the flavour of its
tapering, pale-yellow roots.
Care: Its grows best in light, loamy soil but will
usually grow in all but the heaviest soils. Sow seeds
in April thinly, 1 in deep in 15 ins drills. Thin to 10
ins apart. Hoe regularly and keep well-watered.
Harvesting: Roots will be ready mid-October. Lift
as needed, leaving some in until spring when they
produce tender shoots which can be blanched and
eaten.
Preserving: In boxes of sand in cool, airy place.

VALERIANELLA locusta
Corn salad

Description: A hardy annual grown for its leaves as a salad vegetable. Grows throughout the year but generally sown as an autumn and winter crop when fresh salad material is scarce.

Care: Well-drained soil containing well-rotted manure. Sow in March, April, August and September to keep year-round crop or in August and September for winter crop. Sow in 0.5 in drills, 9 ins apart and thin to 6 ins. Water regularly after sowing and weed. Protect during cold spells.

Harvesting: Ready when fourth leaf pair produced.

Preserving: Not suited.

ZEA mays
Sweet corn

Description: Half hardy annual commonly known as maize and grown for its edible grains in cobs.

Care: Sunny sheltered spot in bed which has been well-manured the winter before planting. Grows best in blocks for cross-pollination. Best sown under glass in April two at a time, 0.5 in deep in 2.5 ins peat pots filled with moist seed compost. Cover with newspaper and glass until germinated. Discard weaker seedlings and place in light. Harden off when 6 ins, plant out in late May 15 ins apart in rows 2 ft apart. Water and feed regularly.

Harvesting: As silky flower tassels turn brown.

Preserving: Bottle and freeze (blanch: 4-6 mins.).

VICIA faba
Broad bean

Description: A hardy, easily cultivated annual grown for its tasty, fat seeds in pods. Tops can be cooked like spinach. There are varieties with many-coloured flowers and varieties with white flowers.

Care: Fertile, well-drained soil dressed with manure. Sow in November for early crop and March or April for main crop. Set seeds 6 ins apart and 1.5-2 ins deep in double row with 9 ins between rows. Allow 2.5 ft between double rows. In an exposed garden will need support. Water well when dry. Sow indoors in January or February. Germination in 2 weeks, plant out in April. For early crop you have to use varieties with many-coloured flowers, for main crop you can use varieties with many-coloured flowers as well as varieties with white flowers. The pods of the varieties with many-coloured flowers get a brown colour when cooked and have a specific taste produced by tannic acid. The pods of the varieties with white flowers stay white or green when cooked.

Harvesting: From June till August. Pick when the beans are still young and juicy.

Preserving: Bottling, freezing (blanch: 3 mins.).

59
FRUITS

Such is the size of most gardens nowadays that the traditional orchard is a far less common sight. Anyone planning fruit trees and bushes needs to pay very careful attention to height and size when they are planning what they will be able to grow. This will have to be done in conjunction with planning all other areas of the garden including shrubs, vegetables and herbs. Details of the height and spread of individual fruit crops are given in the succeeding pages. Fortunately, nowadays, many varieties of fruit which once would take up a large space have been bred in small or dwarf forms and even a small garden can provide a good crop of fruits. When you are planning what you will grow it is advisable to consider the height and spread that any fruit tree or bush will attain when mature – not at the time of planting.

Those with smaller gardens will be looking for a good return on the area of land they allocate. Soft fruits which are borne on bushes, canes and low-growing plants produce crops sooner after planting than top fruits and will, generally speaking, give a better return on land usage. On the other hand, once they mature, top fruits can produce heavy yields. Investigate thoroughly the cropping and the area of land taken up by those crops. Draw a scale plan of your garden marking in the areas your fruits will take up so that you can ensure the best usage. Another important factor to bear in mind is that if you are planning to plant individual fruit trees you will need to select self-fertile varieties.

ACTINIDIA chinensis
Kiwi fruit

Description: Otherwise known as the Chinese gooseberry this is a hardy, decidous climbing shrub. Succulent, hairy, green fruit.
Care: They like any soil. Plant November to March in sunny spot and against wall. Male and female flowers are on separate plants and need to be grown near each other to ensure pollination. Pinch-out growing points when young. Sow seeds in cold greenhouse October and November, prick out into pots in spring. Put established pot plants into outdoor bed until ready for planting out.
Pruning: Thin-out and cut back in February.
Preserving: Bottled in syrup.

ARBUTUS unedo
Strawberry tree

Description: A hardy shrub with orange-red strawberry-like fruit.
Care: Plant trees in October, or from March to May, in lime-free soil and a sunny, sheltered spot. Protect young trees in winter with straw. Sow seeds in March in pans of 2 parts peat to one part sand (by volume) and place in cold frame. Prick-out, when large enough to handle, into 3 ins pots. Grow-on one or two years in cold frame. Transplant to growing site from March to May. Or take heel cuttings 3-4 ins long in July. Propagate at 18°C.
Pruning: None required.
Preserving: Probably not worth it.

CASTANEA sativa
Sweet or Spanish chestnut

Description: Hardy deciduous tree at its best in October and November when the ripe spiny fruits fall to the ground. Nuts can be obtained by carefully prizing open the prickly husks. It flowers in July with erect, pale-green and yellow catkins.
Care: They thrive in good garden soil and should be planted from October to March in an open, sunny position. Sow seeds when ripe, in October, transplanting seedlings the following autumn. Grow-on 3-4 years before planting in permanent site. Will grow to 30 ft eventually.
Pruning: None required.
Preserving: Eat fresh, pickled, boiled or pureed.

CITRUS rutaceae
Citrus

Description: A group of trees and shrubs notable for edible thick-skinned fruits like oranges, lemons, grapefruit and tangerines.
Care: Can be grown here but only as house plants from seed or, for fruits, in hothouse conditions at 18-24°C. Grow in pots of compost keeping them just moist in winter and well-watered in summer. Syringe the leaves daily when hot. Ventilate area in summer and stand in a well-lit position. Remove the top 2 ins of compost annually replacing with a mixture of (by volume) equal parts loam and manure.
Preserving: Bottled.

CORYLUS avellana
Hazel

Description: Hazel is the general name given to
trees of the corylus genus which includes cobnuts
and filberts. Even when grown in bush form they can
take up considerable space. Grows up to 20 ft high
with spread of up to 15 ft.
Care: Plant October to March in well-drained soil,
open sunny site protected from east winds. Propagate by pegging-down layers in autumn, sever when
well-rooted – after about a year – and grow in
nursery bed for 1-2 years before transplanting.
Pruning: Cut-back previous growth by half in early
years.
Preserving: When brown eat or dry in warm place.

CYDONIA oblonga
Quince

Description: This colourful and attractive deciduous branching tree makes a splendid feature.
Care: If growing bushes buy 2-year-old plants and if
standards buy 3-4 year-olds. Plant during late
October or November, in a sunny, open position or
against a sheltered wall. Will succeed in any ordinary
soil but likes loamy, moist soil. Each February apply
bonemeal and in May a mulch.
Pruning: For 3-4 years winter-prune one-year-old
growth by half. None necessary after this but tidy
diseased wood.
Preserving: Pick fruit in October, store in cool
place or freeze (in syrup).

FICUS carica
Fig

Description: Sub-tropical tree, in northern Europe
grown as a bush tree. Needs sun.
Care: Plant in March in a bed which has concrete
slabs to impede root growth beyond 3 ft wide. Place
brick rubble 12 ins deep in bottom of bed and cover
with two parts garden soil to one of mortar rubble
mixed with bonemeal. Cover roots well, firm down
and mulch. For three years train trees up wall or
trellis and in subsequent summers pinch out side
shoots keeping five leaves at end of June. Protect
shoots in winter.
Harvesting: August-October.
Preserving: Bottled or dried.

HIPPOPHAE rhamnoides
Sea buckthorn

Description: A hardy deciduous shrub grown for
its berries and which can sometimes reach a height
of 30 ft, though heights of 10 ft are average. Its
brown, scaly branches are covered with spines and
silver leaves. Tiny yellow flowers develop in April.
The berries are generally very sharp and even the
birds don't eat them.
Care: Easily-grown in ordinary well-drained soil. It
thrives, as the name suggests, in sandy areas near
the sea. Plant in sunny spot from October to February
in groups containing both sexes.
Harvesting: Acrid, unpleasant, orange berries in
autumn and winter.

FRAGARIA ananassa
Strawberry

Description: Strawberries are as much a part of summer as trips to the seaside and back garden barbecues. Mercifully, they are also very easy to grow if the rules are followed properly. They also give the gardener a quicker return for his work than almost any other fruit since they are planted out in late summer and give a crop the following June. By growing a number of carefully selected varieties the strawberry-lover can ensure picking from May to October, using cloches to extend the growing season. Basically, there are two main types of strawberry: those that carry a single crop of fruit in the summer and those that crop at intervals from June to October and which are known as ever-bearing or perpetual. Most varieties are self-fertile but need to be pollinated by insects. Among recommended varieties of single cropping strawberries are 'Grandee', 'Cambridge Rival' and 'Royal Sovereign'. Some perpetual varieties recommended include 'Sans Rivale', 'St Claude' and 'Gento'.
Care: For success in growing strawberries you will need a rich, well-drained soil and a sunny position. Before planting dig in well-rotted manure or compost at the rate of a full bucket to the square yard. Then fork in a good general fertiliser at the rate of 2 oz per square yard. Make sure there is no organic material lying on top of the soil since this will encourage slugs and pests. Grow early crops in a sheltered, sunny border and main crops in an open bed. The flowers are susceptible to frosts and will need to be protected with newspaper when frosts threaten. Plant out as early as possible if growing an early crop, which will need protection from November.
There are two ways of growing strawberries. They can be grown as single plants with all the runners removed or as rows with the runners rooting all the way along. Whichever system is used, and this will depend on the wetness of your plot since the former method is best in damp spots, make sure you use certified stock or runners taken from healthy plants.

If planting has to be delayed until March or April remove the flowers so plants get established for cropping the next year. Plant the perpetuals no later than August or wait until March or April.
Set plants 18 ins apart in rows 2.5 ft apart, spreading the roots so that the base of the plant is level with the surface. Scatter slug pellets when berries begin to form and place fresh straw under each plant to keep fruit off the ground. You can also use black polythene or strawberry mats now sold in shops. To protect from birds cover with netting. On single cropping varieties loosen the straw and set fire to it to destroy pests and old leaves. Do not burn perpetual varieties, this will kill off new growth. Just remove old leaves and burn. In late September-early October cover perpetuals with cloches for late crops and in January rake-in sulphate of potash at 1.5 oz per square yard. Strawberries can also be grown solely under glass using plant-pot grown runners or in special barrels now sold in garden centres or shops.
Stocks can be increased from runners which are produced in large amounts by plants from June onwards. Propagate by layering the runners. Select three or four strong ones from each, peg into the soil and pinch off outer end of the runner. After 4-6 weeks the new plant should be well-rooted. Sever and set in growing position. The ability of all strawberry plants to produce the maximum amount of yield soon diminishes and they should be renewed at least every 4-5 years. Burn old plants and set new ones on a fresh site. Pests and diseases which will attack your plants include aphids, cutworms, glasshouse red spider mite, slugs, snails, strawberry beetle and strawberry mite, grey mould, leaf spot and powdery mildew.
Harvesting: Strawberries should be picked by the stalk to avoid bruising and they should be eaten as soon as possible after picking.
Preserving: Strawberries are best fresh and nothing you can do to them will match this taste but they can also be bottled in syrup, made into jams and frozen (pureed or in syrup).

JUGLANS regia
Walnut

Description: Hardy, deciduous tree grown for its timber and edible nuts.
Care: Will reach 25 ft high and 15 ft spread comfortably and may eventually grow to 100 ft high. Plant October to March while young in fertile, well-drained soil in an open position. Protect from spring frosts and mulch with manure annually in spring until well-established. Can be propagated from seed sown in October to November in nursery rows outdoors. Grow on for 3-4 years before putting in permanent site. Avoid pruning.
Harvesting: Gather nuts after they drop.
Preserving: Pickled or in sand with salt.

MALUS Rosaceae
Crab apple

Description: Grown largely as an ornamental tree, this relative of the apple nevertheless has an edible fruit which is still used for making jams and preserves. It needs little pruning and is much less trouble to grow than dessert and cooking apples.
Care: Well-drained, fertile soil dressed with rotted manure. Plant in autumn or winter and tie to a stake until established. Water well if dry the spring after planting. It wil be self-fertile so only grow one tree.
Harvesting: September and October.
Preserving: Jams and wine.

MESPILUS germanica
Medlar

Description: Another tree which may be too large for the average garden growing to 20 ft high and a spread of 20 ft. Edible fruits and a statuesque ornamental appearance make it a real garden feature.
Care: Loamy, well-drained soil in sunny spot which is sheltered from north and easterly winds. Buy a 3-4 year-old standard or half standard and plant in well-manured soil October to March.
Pruning: Prune back leaders of main branches by half each winter for two years then by a quarter for two years. Cut strong side shoots to 6 ins.
Harvesting: October to November.
Preserving: In preserves and jellies.

MORUS nigra
Mulberry

Description: Grown as much for leaves as for the fruit since they are the sole food of silkworms. Hardy, deciduous, slow-growing tree reaching 20 ft high with a 15 ft spread.
Care: Buy young tree from nursery and plant in open, sunny position in well-manured soil. If hard to find take a 12 ins long cutting from a tree, with two-year-old wood at the base, in autumn or early spring. Plant deeply, with all but 2-3 buds buried, in nursery bed until well-rooted.
Pruning: Dead wood only. Avoid heavy pruning.
Harvesting: Shake tree gently into a sheet beneath.
Preserving: Bottled or frozen (dry, syrup, pureed).

PRUNUS
Introduction

A group of related species which covers 430 types. To the gardener the group contains some of the most appealing spring flowering ornamentals to be found. Probably the most popular, and hailed as the queen of the spring-blooming trees, is the flowering cherry – a variety of prunus which reaches about 20 ft when mature and which boasts heavy clusters of five-petalled white or pink flowers between March and May. Flowering cherries, as they are commonly called, also include a bewildering assortment of varieties and are usually grouped into four main categories – almond, plum, peach and cherry. Nearly all of these are easy to grow in soil which is reasonably fertile and well-drained.

Varieties of almond include 'Alba' which has white flowers, 'Erecta' with a narrow column-like growth for the small garden. The common almond (P. duclis and P. amygdalus) grows to about 25 ft high and has pink flowers in March. Perhaps the most beautiful is P. amygdalo-persica 'Pollardii' which bears rich pink flowers in March and April. Varieties of plum include 'Nigra' which has pink flowers and blackish leaves. The cherry plum (P. cerasifera) can be grown as a hedge or spreading tree. Purplish or coppery foliage is a common feature. The peaches are a bit more temperamental than most varieties of prunus and can be a little short-lived. They need shelter and are susceptible to leaf curl. The Chinese peach (P. davidiana) gives early single pink blooms in January. The choice and variety of the cherry is quite bewildering and it would pay you to consult a knowledgeable assistant at the garden centre or shop before buying an unknown one. Most popular are the Japanese cherries like 'Amanogawa' (20 ft, pink flowers in May) and the weeping variety 'Kikushidare Sakura' (15 ft, pink flowers in April). In the ordinary cherry group can be found the bird cherry (P. padus) which grows to 20 ft and has almond-scented white flowers in May, and the wild cherry (P. avium) which grows to 40 ft and boasts white flowers in April and bark which is itself an ornamental feature.

There is a fifth section – lesser known and not as common – cherry laurels. The laurels are evergreens and useful for large hedges and screens. They grow up to 20 ft high and 30 ft across and varieties include the common laurel (P. laurocerasus) which bears white flowers in April and makes an outstanding hedging shrub, and Portugal laurel (P. lusitanica) which has creamy, highly scented flowers in June. Most varieties of prunus are shallow-rooting and don't like being planted too deeply. Most will thrive in ordinary soil but don't like it either too dry or too wet. If the site is windy or exposed standard specimen trees will need firm staking until they are established, while in areas which are likely to have visits from animals it may be necessary to protect the base with chicken wire in winter.

To propagate it is generally best to grow from seed but some varieties can be successfully increased by vegetative propagation. Seed-raised trees can be longer-lived though in places where different species grow and flower together hybrids are likely to arise. Smaller flowering species can be increased by taking heel cuttings 3-4 ins long in July. Insert in peat and sand of equal parts by volume, place in propagating tray at 18°C, pot when rooted into 3 ins pots and overwinter in cold frame. Grow-on in nursery bed the following spring and for 1-2 years to get established before planting out.

With the ornamental almonds no regular pruning should be necessary but old flowering shoots on some varieties may need to be cut back to within two or three buds of the base after flowering. The ornamental peach needs no regular pruning. Ornamental plums need little regular attention but hedge varieties will need to be clipped at any convenient time during the year, but if they are being grown for the flowers then this should be delayed until the flowering period is over. Prune back the old flowering shoots. Ornamental cherries in the hedging varieties will need to be clipped immediately after flowering while large branches may need to be removed, and this should be done in late summer. Cherry laurels, grown generally for their hedging qualities, will need to be cut back hard into the old wood in March or April.

PRUNUS armeniaca
Apricot

Description: A native of China best-grown in northern Europe as an espalier against warm-sheltered walls.
Care: Well-drained lime rich soil. From November to March plant 2-3 year-old trees which should fruit when four. Train up wall or trellis. Top dress soil each winter with bonemeal and sulphate of potash and every third year omit the bonemeal, using instead manure or compost. Protect blossoms from frost with nylon mesh and assist pollination with camel hair brush.
Pruning: In early spring as growth begins.
Preserving: Bottled, dried, frozen (syrup, pureed).

PRUNUS cerasus
Acid cherry, morello

Description: A less vigorous grower than the sweet cherry it is grown as a bush or espalier, and its fruit is ideal for bottling and jam-making.
Care: Plant espalier varieties at four years and bush varieties at two, from November to February. Will grow in ordinary, well-drained soil in an open spot. Grown in bare soil free of weeds. Apply sulphate of ammonia and of potash in spring and water regularly in summer especially when growing up walls. Cut fruit off trees with scissors.
Pruning: Shorten young leaders in winter. Reduce pruning until, at four years, it is slight.
Preserving: Bottled and jam.

PRUNUS avium
Sweet cherry

Description: The Prunus avium comes from the countries around the Black and Caspian Seas. It has white, sometimes pinky red flowers, that have no green leaves at the end of the flower clusters. Sweet cherry trees need a lot of space. In addition, you will need to plant two trees because cross-pollination is necessary to fertilise the flowers. Among the best known varieties are the 'Biggereau Napoleon' (a hard cherry with a poor, slightly sharp taste), the 'Early Rivers' (a soft, dark brown cherry with a good flavour), the 'Inspecteur Löhnis' (a late cherry with dark brown, fairly solid, sweet tasting fruit), the 'Wijnkers' (a shiny, dark brown cherry with a soft, juicy fruit) and the 'Schneiders Späte Knor-pelkirsche' (a large, red-brown cherry with hard, crisp and juicy fruit). The 'Maycherry' is also counted among the sweet cherries. Actually, it is a hybrid; a cross of the Prunus avium with the Prunus cerasus. The Fruit of the 'Maycherry' is not large, round and dark red; the flesh is soft and rather sharp.
Care: The sweet cherry needs well-drained, fertile ground. Plant a two-year full size or half standard tree between November and February. Remember that most cherries are strong growers: plant them at a distance of 13 ft apart. Only the needs less space. Cherries can burst, especially during rain; but fairly safe from this are the 'Wijnkers' and the 'Maycherry'. In addition, cherries can be attacked by Monilia rot; brown flecks with grey raised tracks in concentric circles on the fruit. Cherries that have burst are extra sensitive for Monilia.
Pruning: As long as the tree is still young, the shoots mst be cut back to half their length. After 4 years pruning becomes more or less unnecessary. It can be limited to thinning cut in summer to ensure that the sunlight can penetrate.
Harvesting: June-July.
Preserving: Deep freeze, jams.

PRUNUS domestica
Plum

Introduction

A group of hardy trees and shrubs grown for their edible fruits and which often take from four to six years to start cropping. Not suitable for small gardens and can only be satisfactorily trained as espaliers. Should not be planted in cold or exposed sites because they flower early. A rough guide for planting distances would be: bushes–15 ft, half-standards–18 ft, standards–20 ft and espaliers – 15 - 18 ft.

Plums do best in deep, well-drained heavy loams. Maiden trees should be planted in autumn, staked and placed in bare soil to reduce the competition for moisture in summer. Do not bury the union between rootstock and scion or it will from its own rootstock. Water, mulch, to retain moisture in summer, and dress with nitrogen. Established trees should also be dressed with sulphate of ammonia annually and, every 2-3 years, superphosphate. Plums are shallow-rooting so do not cultivate site deeply. Leave dessert fruits to ripen on the tree and pick carefully. Propagate by budding in July/ August or by grafting in March. Prune young trees in early spring and mature ones in summer.

The most common pests and diseases include birds, aphids, plum sawfly, bacterial canker, brown rot, honey fungus, shot hole and silver leaf.

PRUNUS domestica
Plum 'Czar'

Description: The 'Czar' is an English plum. It is a strong grower with a steep tree shape. By grafting the 'Czar' onto the 'St. Julian A' its growth can be checked. The fruit is fairly small, oval in shape and purple-blue in colour. The 'Czar' has sweet tasting fruit.
Care: As given in the general introduction.
Harvesting: August.
Preserving: Jams or frozen.

PRUNUS domestica
Plum 'Damson'

Description: The 'Damson' comes from the countryside around Damascus, thus its name. Some varieties have precious little fruit and too much stone. Try 'Bradley's King', a dessert or cooking variety or 'Cheshire Damson' which is ideal for bottling. Generally speaking they are smaller than plums although they come from the same family.
Care: They succeed in poor soils where other fruits won't grow and are often hardy enough to grow in northern areas where more tender ones will not survive. Most are self-fertile. Grow as for plums.
Harvesting: When soft and jucy. Pick by the stalk.
Preserving: Bottled, wine.

PRUNUS domestica
Plum 'Early Laxton'

Description: A large, ovoid-fruiting plum which turns golden yellow and has a good, fleshy taste.
Care: Should grow in any site favourable to plums. Follow instructions set out in the general introduction to plums.
Harvesting: The 'Early Laxton' is a heavy cropper and the branches may need some support to avoid splitting. Starts to produce ripe fruit in July.
Preserving: Bottled or frozen (sugar, syrup, puree).

PRUNUS domestica
Plum 'Ontario'

Description: 'Ontario' is a very productive, self fertile variety. The fruit is large and greenish-yellow in colour and has a sweet flavour.
Care: 'Ontario' can be grown just as well under glass as outdoors. Outside the growth will be moderate. For good pollination it is recommended that when it blooms the flowers are dusted with a small soft brush. Thin out the fruit in June and prune in September.
Harvesting: Under glass in July. Outdoors in August.
Preserving: Best used fresh.

PRUNUS domestica
Greengage

Description: A variety of plum which, while often having a much better taste, can be more difficult to grow. Usually the varieties will be less hardy than plums. Try 'Cambridge Gage', which matures in mid to late August. It has a splendid taste and is suitable for both dessert and bottling. Unfortunately, like most gages, it can produce poor crops from its own pollen and will need to be grown with other plum varieties like 'Laxton's Gage'.
Care: As for plums.
Harvesting: Not quite ripe (bottling) or ripen on the tree if eating fresh.
Preserving: Bottled, frozen.

PRUNUS domestica
Plum 'Reine Victoria'

Description: A bright red plum with darker speckles which is good for bottling, jam-making and desserts. Its growth, however, is brittle and, as a result, can lead to splitting, Self-fertile, it is a good cropper. Can be susceptible to silver leaf. Flowers in mid-season.
Care: Espalier varieties should be grown up a north- or west-facing wall. Firm back in if lifted by frost. Reduce danger of splitting, and thus silver leaf, by supporting branches with stakes to take weight of crops, and also thin crop to 2-3 ins.
Preserving: Jam, bottled, frozen (sugar, syrup, puree).

PRUNUS dulcis
Almond

Description: A vigorous tree which has firm erect branches when young and spreads out later. Height 18 ft, spread up to 25 ft. Mid-green leaves and almost translucent pink flowers 1-2 ins across in March and April. It comes in forms 'Alba' which has white flowers and 'Rosea-plena' which has double pale pink flowers. Makes an excellent ornamental tree but in these climes you cannot expect to see good quality nuts.
No pruning is necessary except in pruning dead wood and leaves.
Harvesting: Fruits will be inedible.
Preserving: Not applicable.

PRUNUS institia
Black cherry, mirabelle, bullace

Description: A moderate grower, reaching up to 20 ft in height. Bears small round fruit, the colour of which varies from yellow to blue-black. The best known varieties are 'Yellow Black Cherry', 'Mirabelle de Nancy' and 'Mirabelle de Metz'.
Care: 'Mirabelle de Nancy' is the easiest to grow. The tree is very suitable for small gardens, productive, self-fertile and provides a tasty fruit. It is not particularly susceptible to diseases. The fruit should be thinned out in June, and the tree must be pruned in September.
Harvesting: August to September.
Preserving: In jams or syrups.

PRUNUS persica
Peach

Description: A hardy, deciduous tree which bears fruit with hairy skin and stones. Early-flowering so needs protection against spring frosts.
Care: Needs sheltered, sunny spot and ideally should be grown as an espalier against a south-facing wall or fence or under glass. Only succeeds in well-drained soil. Plant October to January with roots well spaced and 9 ins from base of wall. Feed in January with sulphate of potash and in March with nitro-chalk.
Pruning: Thin fruits to 9 ins.
Preserving: Bottled, dried, frozen (sugar, syrup, puree).

PRUNUS persica
Nectarine

Description: Smooth-skinned form of the peach which is less hardy and which will need a well-sheltered site if it is to grow outdoors.
Care: Plant maiden trees in late October erect windbreaks and leave stem 9 ins from wall. Plant in greenhouse but leave minimum span of 10 ft. If growing outdoors protect flowers from frosts with hessian. Pollinate with camel hair brush, especially if grown under glass. Water outdoors as necessary and regularly under glass. Thin fruits to 9 ins when the size of nuts.
Harvesting: Pluck in palm of hand, carefully.
Preserving: Bottled, frozen (sugar, syrup, puree).

PYRUS communis
Pear

Introduction

Hardy deciduous trees which flower in spring and bear edible fruits in late summer and autumn. They fruit earlier than the apple and thus need a warmer site which will help to improve the quality of the fruit. If grown properly they are generally easier to bring to fruit than the apple but those living in the most northerly areas may find they simply cannot get pears to succeed. More tolerant of poor drainage than apples they are, however, less able to get by without moisture. They succeed best in fertile, water-retaining loams.

Pears should be grown in a sunny, sheltered spot in deep, loamy soil which will retain as much moisture as possible in summer without making the area too heavy. If the soil is likely to be too well-drained then, before planting, dig two or three buckets of peat into it. Also, before planting fork in a general fertiliser at the rate of around 3 oz per square yard. In subsequent years top dress the area, over the full root spread, with sulphate of potash at the rate of 1 oz per square yard. In March apply 1.5 oz of sulphate of ammonia per square yard and every third year add 2 oz superphosphate to your ammonia top dressing.

Yields for pear trees can vary significantly according to weather and variety but here is a rough guide. From a well-established cordon you should get up to 5 lb; from a dwarf pyramid you should get up to 6 lb; up to 25 lb from a good-cropping three-tier espalier and as much as 50 lbs from a mature bush tree.

Plant the trees between November and March, staking them to ensure steady growth, and making sure that the tree is planted to the same depth as it was in the nursery. This will be indicated by a soil mark on the stem. Also make sure that the joint between stock and scion is kept well above the soil level. Spread the roots out evenly and firm back the soil. During the winter frosts may well lift the tree so firm it back. Water during dry weather and mulch with well-rotted compost. Do not plant when the soil is either frozen or very wet and while waiting store the trees in a frost-free shed.

Usually the pear tree will need less thinning than apples but some will still be necessary and should be carried out at the end of June. When cropping well reduce each cluster to one or two small fruits just as they begin to turn downwards.

Most varieties of pear will ripen off the tree but leave fruits of all but the earliest varieties to mature as long as possible on the tree. Harvest only when the pear twists easily from the tree. An exception to this rule is the early varieties like 'Williams Bon Chrétien' which should be picked before it has fully ripened on the tree.

In the early years most pear trees will be pruned in much the same way as apple trees. Once they become established, however, it may be necessary to put in far more work. Overcrowded branches will need to be removed, and generally the pear tree is cut back much harder. This is especially true in the centre of the tree during winter pruning.

Unfortunately the pear tree is attacked by a great variety of pests and diseases. Birds will peck at the ripening fruit and at the flower buds in the winter. Aphids are likely to infest young shoots, making them sticky and damaging the young leaves. Pear leaf blister mites can attack leaf tissues and young fruit producing yellow or brown blisters. Apple canker shows up as oval diseased areas on the bark. Brown rot will cause the fruit to decay rapidly both on the tree and when stored. Eye rot is a rotting, first at the eye end and then spreading to the whole fruit. Fireblight affects the flowers which blacken and shrivel and, finally, pear scab produces brown or black scabs on the fruit. Although the pear tree is affected by many of the same problems as the apple tree, it tends to be more resistant and any spraying programme will have to take account of this. A proper programme of spraying will deal with most of these problems but do not spray when the blossom is fully open. Over-spraying can do more harm than good by killing off many beneficial insects. Also apply tar-oil every third year during the dormant period, this should control aphids, scale insects and other problems.

PYRUS communis
Pear 'Beurré Alexandre Lucas'

Description: The 'Beurré Alexandre Lucas' comes from France. It is a fairly large tree, pyramid in shape with limp, downward hanging branches. The fruit is large, fat and green; when it ripens it turns yellow. The fruit is sweet and juicy.
Care: The pollen of the 'Beurré Alexandre Lucas' is sterile. To fertilise, the pollen of another variety, for example the 'Bonne Louise d'Avrache', can be used.
Harvesting: September. If you want to store the fruit, it is advisable to pick it earlier.
Preserving: Jam or dried.

PYRUS communis
Pear 'Beurré Hardy'

Description: Medium to large conical, and often uneven, fruit but a splendid white juicy flesh inside a yellowish-green skin, which will be littered with a fine-brown russet spot and sometimes a carmine flush.
Care: As for other pears listed in the general introduction, can sometimes be a disappointing cropper and may be slow to start producing but will grow vigorous and upright.
Harvesting: Mid to late-October. Pick when hard and ripen-off in store.
Preserving: Bottled and dried.

PYRUS communis
Pear 'Bonne Louise d'Avrache'

Description: The 'Bonne Louise' is a tall, thin tree, very suitable as an espalier. The fruit is small and has a green colour with a russett blush. It is juicy and rather sharp.
Care: Fertilisation can be achieved by cross-pollination with, for example, the 'Beurré Hardy', the 'Conférence' or the 'Doyenné du Comice'. Its productivity is irregular, and in fruitful years the pears should be thinned out to encourage growth.
Harvesting: September.
Preserving: Jam, compote.

PYRUS communis
Pear 'Clapp's Favourite'

Description: A less frequently cultivated pear than many varieties but perhaps it has been unfairly ignored by growers. It has a vigorous upright growth and is generally a reliable, heavy-bearer. A sweet, fresh taste.
Care: Because of its vigorous growth it can be inclined to suffer badly from scab in moist climates. When pruning it is important to have the buds facing outwards. Other growing methods are as for pears in the previous instructions.
Harvesting: When almost ripe of using for freezing or for bottling. Otherwise allow it to ripen on the tree.
Preserving: Bottled or frozen.

PYRUS communis
Pear 'Conférence'

Description: A reliable cropper even when frosts occur. It has a sweet, creamy-white firm flesh. Long, thin, tapering fruit, dark almost olive-green skin with brown russet. Suitable for growing in northern regions where some other pears may not survive.
Care: As for other pears in general introduction. It will flower in mid-season and is pollinated by 'Williams Bon Chrétien' and 'Josephine de Malines'.
Harvesting: Pick in September for eating in October and November.
Preserving: Especially good for bottling.

PYRUS communis
Pear 'Doyenné du Comice'

Description: An excellently flavoured pear with a delicate white flesh that almost melts in the mouth. Medium to large fruit, greenish-yellow skin with a brownish-red flush.
Care: This is a pear which demands far more than most but the results are worth it. It needs shelter, rich soil, regular mulching and does not like late frosts. Pollinated by 'Williams Bon Chrétien' and 'Conference' it flowers late and is susceptible to scab.
Harvesting: October for eating late October to December.
Preserving: Best fresh but bottled or dried.

PYRUS communis
Pear 'Souvenir du Congres'

Description: This is a variety of pear which has not been commonly grown particularly as people have tended to have smaller gardens. It will not succeed when grafted to the traditional quince stock – the method for producing small trees which suit the smaller, modern garden. But if you have a large garden then there is no reason why you should not grow it.
Care: As for other pears in this section.
Harvesting: It ripens in September.
Preserving: Bottled, frozen or stored.

PYRUS communis
Pear 'Triomphe de Vienne'

Description: The 'Triomphe de Vienne' is a wide tree with long branches, very suitable as an espalier. The fruit is regular in shape, green to bronze in colour, juicy and sweet.
Care: Fertilisation can be achieved by cross-pollination with, for example, the 'Bonne Louise d'Avranche'. In fruitful years, thin out the pears to encourage growth. This variety is sensitive to scab and pear gall fly.
Harvesting: September.
Preserving: The 'Triomphe de Vienne' is difficult to preserve; possibly as jam or syrup.

PYRUS malus
Apple

Introduction

Apples do not grow well in coastal areas or in the most northerly parts where there is a greater risk of the blossom being destroyed by frosts. For the greatest chance of success in cold northerly areas plant late-flowering culinary or frost resistant dessert varieties.

Apple trees grow best in open, sunny but sheltered spots and will grow well in all but the most water-logged soils. If planting prepare the site the previous September by digging into the soil well-rotted manure at the rate of a bucketful to the square yard. Also apply a general fertiliser at the rate of 3 oz to the square yard.

For most people one apple tree will be enough but others will want to sample a variety. Bush trees, planted at 12-20 ft apart, are fine if there is plenty of space and one mature bush tree could produce as much as 200 lbs of fruit. But if the space is more restricted then try one or two dwarf-pyramid trees which can be spaced at about 6 ft apart. One of these should crop at around 15 lbs per season. An espalier, with a spread of up to 15 ft, can be grown against a wall or trellis, while single-stemmed cordons can be trained up wires. When fully-established the cordons could crop at as much as 10 lbs a season. When choosing the variety of apple tree it would be wise to consult your garden centre or shop. Only good local knowledge and experience will be able to tell you just what sort of site and soil will best suit the type you choose. Most apple trees will not pollinate themselves and so you can grow varieties with overlapping blossoming periods for cross-pollination.

The best time to plant apple trees is during frost-free weather between November and March. They like well-drained deep soil that will not dry out in the summer. If necessary dig in organic matter to improve the soil. Dig a hole large enough to take the roots when they are spread out and before planting drive in a stake and put the tree up against it. Keep the union between stock and scion at least 4 ins above the soil level. In the first growing season keep it well-watered in any dry spells and in the spring of the three following years mulch with compost or manure to keep moisture in the soil. In January dress with 1 oz of sulphate of potash per square yard and every third year add 2 oz of superphosphate to this dressing. In March dress with sulphate of ammonia at 2 oz per square yard for cookers and 1 oz for others. All dressings should cover fully the area of the branch spread.

For espaliers, buy a three-year-old tree which should have two tiers already trained by the nurseryman. Plant and tie up branches to support wires. Cut back the main stem to a bud 2 ins above the wire that will support the next tier above. As growth begins pick two good buds below the cut on opposite sides of the stem, which will grow into side branch. Rub out any buds between these three. Now you should have two tiers growing sideways and the main stem growing upwards. Tie a cane vertically to the support wires and tie the centre shoot to it as it grows. Attach two more canes, at 45 degree angles, to the centre cane and tie side shoots to these as they grow. The next winter remove side canes, lower the branches and tie them to the third tier of support wires. This way you develop an established tree of three tiers. When tiers have reached desired length, cut back previous year's growth to 0.5 in each May. In late July to August prune shoots from the tiers to three leaves from the basal cluster and shoots from the laterals to one leaf.

To train a cordon, prune when the new summer growth matures – when shoots are at least 9 ins long. Cut back from the main stem to three leaves beyond the basal cluster and prune shoots from laterals or spurs leaving one leaf. When a cordon grows beyond the top support wire, untie and re-fasten at a more acute angle and lower neighbouring cordons so they remain parallel. When it reaches its final height cut back new growth on the leader to 0.5 in in May. Cut above a bud and repeat the process each May. A dwarf pyramid is trained to a shape like a Christmas tree by pruning the central leader to leave about 9 ins of new growth. Branch leaders are pruned to about 7 ins. Then in the summer, shorten mature growth on branch leaders to 5 or 6 leaves above the basal cluster. Prune laterals to three leaves beyond basal cluster and spurs to one leaf beyond. Each winter shorten central leader. When it reaches 7 ft cut back half the previous summer's growth on the central leader each May.

PYRUS manus
Apple 'Cox's Orange Pippin'

Description: Generally held to be the finest
flavoured of all dessert apples and consequently
expensive to buy in the shops. A crisp bite and
tender, yellow juicy flesh. Round, conical, regular-
sized fruit, golden-yellow with a brownish-red flush.
Medium-sized tree with upright, slender branches.
Care: As for apples in general introduction. The
blossoms are not hardy and the tree can develop
canker in cold and wet soils. It is also susceptible to
scab and mildew which makes it a difficult fruit to
grow.
Harvesting: October to December.
Preserving: Stored, bottled, dried, frozen.

PYRUS malus
Apple 'Discovery'

Description: Crisp, sweet and juicy early apple
which unfortunately is liked as much by the birds and
wasps as it is by the rest of us. It is a small to
medium-sized apple greenish-yellow in colour but
covered over a large part of the surface with bright
red. A good, regular cropper which may be slow to
bear.
Care: Improve bearing by ensuring it is on a good
rootstock. It has some resistance to scab and is spur-
forming. Its blossom is reasonably tolerant to frosts.
Harvesting: End of August to mid-September.
Preserving: Bottled, dried, frozen.

PYRUS malus
Apple 'Egremont Russet'

Description: A splendid, nutty, distinctive russet
which is hardy, a regular cropper and is probably one
of the best russets for the average garden. The fruit is
a medium yellow colour usually almost covered in
russet. Compact growth.
Care: It should be resistant to the scab which affects
some russets. It flowers early but the blossom is
fairly frost tolerant.
Harvesting: Pick in late September for use in
October to December.
Preserving: Best eaten fresh.

PYRUS malus
Apple 'Golden Delicious'

Description: Probably the most cultivated variety of
apple because of its good shelf life and popularity in
the shops. The fruit are smallish, round, oblong and
slightly ribbed.
Care: General cultivation techniques given in the
introduction to apples apply here. The 'Golden
Delicious' is relatively easy to grow, should be a
reliable cropper and is both hardy and spur-forming.
Can be cross-pollinated by 'Golden Noble', 'Orlean's
Reinette', and 'Howgate Wonder'.
Harvesting: Pick in mid-October for use November
to January.
Preserving: Best eaten fresh.

PYRUS malus
Apple 'James Grieve'

Description: Recommended as a good September apple but it is one which can be prone to bruising and canker. It has an excellent juicy flavour and will be a crisp bite. Medium to large pale-yellow fruit with crimson blotches. Its early fruit can be picked green for cooking.
Care: Its blossom has some tolerance to frost and it should be hardy and reliable as a cropper. Spur forming.
Harvesting: Pick in early September and eat in September to Otober.
Preserving: Bottled, dried, frozen.

PYRUS malus
Apple Jonathan

Description: A winter dessert apple which has been out of favour with growers until fairly recently because it was inclined to be small, show a poor colour and it was susceptible to powdery mildew and Jonathan Spot, tiny sunken spots on the skin. All problems have been worked upon by the experts.
Care: As for apples in the general introduction but note that special precautions may have to be taken to protect against disease.
Harvesting: Pick just after Cox's and can even be left hanging until November. Cold stores safely until March.
Preserving: Bottled or frozen.

PYRUS malus
Apple 'Spartan'

Description: A mid-season apple with a sweet, pleasant, distinctive flavour. The fruit are medium-sized, oblong and yellow, though they may be almost entirely covered with a rich red bloom. It should be a regular and reliable cropper.
Care: The tree is moderately vigorous, growing upright and then spreading. It may be subject to canker though it should be frost tolerant. Spur-forming.
Harvesting: Pick in early October for use in November to January.
Preserving: Bottled, dried, frozen.

PYRUS malus
Apple 'Worcester Pearmain'

Description: One of the best-known and most loved of mid-season apples, this is a crisp, sweet, regular cropper with a slightly chewy texture. It has an upright, and then spreading, growth.
Care: It is inclined to tip-bearing and may be susceptible to scab though it should be resistant to mildew. The blossom should be fairly frost-tolerant.
Harvesting: Pick in early September for use in September to October.
Preserving: Bottled, dried and frozen.

RIBES
Introduction

Black currants, red currants and white currants are all hardy, deciduous shrubs which grow well in temperate areas. They are easy to grow and long-lived which makes them an economic crop in which to invest. The black currant originates from the Ribes nigrum and bears the majority of its crop on growth from the previous year. Varieties of both red and white currants fruit on short spurs which are carried on old wood and the lower parts of the previous year's growth.

All currants can be grown in most moisture-retaining soils but hate poor drainage. They like open, sunny positions but don't like late spring frosts.

Red and white currants are grown as cordons, standards or bushes while black currants are usually only grown as bushes.

Plant October to March staking red and white currants if grown as cordons. Firm bushes after any frosts and mulch in spring with well-rotted compost. Pull out any suckers growing up from below ground. Water in dry spells and in March feed black currants with sulphate of ammonia over root area at the rate of 1.5 oz per square yard.

In February and March red currants and white currants can be given a dressing of sulphate of potash.

All currants can be propagated by taking hardwood cuttings from the healthy wood in the autumn. For black currants take them 10 ins long and 14 ins long for red and white currants.

After planting black currants encourage the root growth by cutting them down to 3 ins above ground level. When mature, if the growth has been vigorous, cut back most of the old dark wood that fruited. Otherwise cut back by one third in the autumn. With red and white currants cut back the previous season's growth by half in the winter of planting. After that cut back the roots by one-third.

Black currant gall mites can cause big bud and virus disease. Birds eat currant buds in winter. Aphids will attack young shoots. The American gooseberry mildew infests shoot tips. Coral spot hits red currants causing them to wither and even die completely. Grey mould causes rotted berries. Honey fungus can kill the plants. Silver leaf can hit red and black currants causing them to die off.

RIBES nigrum
Black currant

Description: The dark, acid berries are richer in nutritious vitamin C than any other garden fruit and can be used for refreshing and medicinal drinks.
Care: Select certified, disease-free plants and place in full sunshine if possible. Enrich soil with compost. Plant bushes 5-6 ft apart and deeper than they were in the nursery. After pruning, bushes will give no fruit the first summer. Instead vigorous new growth will be developed for cropping in the second summer. A mature bush will yield around 12-15 lbs of fruit.
Harvesting: Pick only when really ripe.
Preserving: Jam, bottled, frozen.

RIBES species
Red currant

Description: Smaller than black currants.
Care: Grow well in ordinary soil but hate heavy, badly drained soil so improve with manure containing straw. A good supply of potash is needed to colour the berries and produce firm wood and healthy leaves. Give them a good 6 ft space when planting bushes, and 18 ins for single stemmed cordons. Keep bushes to one clean stem of about 6 ins before allowing branches to form. Remove all suckers and buds below that point.
Harvesting: Pick when ripe and use immediately.
Preserving: Jam, bottled, frozen.

RIBES species
White currant

Description: Not as commonly grown as black or red currants but just as tasty in their own way. It can be grown as a bush, cordon, or even espalier.
Care: As for red currants. Propagation is from hardwood cuttings taken in autumn when the rooting is usually quick. Select strong healthy bushes and take one-year-old growth. Both red and white currants need to be grown on a clean stem and all buds, with the exception of 4 or 5 at the top, should be removed from cuttings.
Harvesting: Handle white currants with care because they bruise easily.
Preserving: Jam, bottled, frozen.

ROSA canina
Rose-hip, dog rose

Description: The rose-hip is the fruit of the dog rose which can be found in abundance in wild hedgerows. Orange-red and about one in long they are rich in vitamin C, containing 20 times as much as an orange.
Care: It grows to a height of up to 8 ft and with a spread of up to 6 ft and is widely used as the rootstock for modern roses. Will grow in most well-drained soil in a sunny spot. Dig in plenty of well-rotted manure and top dress with peat. Plant in October or November.
Harvesting: Late-autumn.
Preserving: In syrup.

RIBES uva-crispa
Gooseberry

Description: Native to northern Europe but only really popular in Britain, the fruit of this hardy shrub is magnificent fresh or in pies, fools, tarts, crumbles and a range of other dishes.
Care: Plant two or three-year-old bushes in November to March in well-drained but moisture retaining soil. Thrives in full sun or partial shade but doesn't like late spring frosts or strong summer winds. Normally they are grown as bushes but they can also be grown as cordons. In this case support with 6 ft high stakes. Firm the roots, especially after frosts. In spring mulch with a well-rotted compost to avoid any danger of drying out, and water during any dry spells between May and July to help new bushes become established and mature ones to feed swelling fruit. In winter feed with sulphate of potash and in March add sulphate of ammonia at 1 oz per square yard.
In April protect from late spring frosts with fine netting or muslin. As the fruits begin to swell you will need to thin them out using the immature berries for cooking or bottling. Ripen the remainder and use them for eating when they are red or yellow (according to the variety).
Initially gooseberries are best grown from stock bought disease free and certified from a reputable garden shop or nursery. They are prone to virus disease but existing stock can be increased from hardwood cuttings taken in October. Take 15 ins long cuttings and remove all but the top five buds. Place 6 ins deep in nursery bed outdoors. Grow-on for a year and plant-out rooted cuttings the following November to March.
Gooseberries are prone to gooseberry sawfly, American gooseberry mildew, cluster cup rust, capsid bugs, grey mould, honey fungus and leaf spot. The biggest threat, however, may well be birds, especially bullfinches, which eat the buds in winter.
Recommended varieties: dessert: 'Keepsake', 'Golden Drop', 'White Lion'; cooking: 'Careless'.
Pruning: Hard pruning of cordons and bushes improves the size of the fruit and keeps older bushes vigorous. Aim first to build up a good shape, then to keep a supply of young growths forming fruiting spurs.
Harvesting: July.
Preserving: Bottled, frozen.

RUBUS
Introduction

Although none of the plants in this family, which includes blackberry, raspberry, loganberry and wineberry, are fussy about where they grow, they will all appreciate good drainage and a rich humus. In preparing the ground it will repay the gardener to dig deeply and fork in some decayed manure adding a seaweed fertiliser or fish meal to provide long term nourishment. Unless the soil contains lime an additional dressing of hydrated lime at the rate of 4 oz per square yard will benefit the plants. With raspberries a lack of potash will show itself by scorched edges to the leaves and is a sign that you should be dressing the soil with a good organic fertiliser and perhaps sulphate of potash sprinkled along the sides of the rows, but not on the canes. Blackberries are usually supplied as healthy one-year old plants and should be planted immediately unless the soil is 'sticky'. With loganberries make sure you have good vigorous stock. Too often poor fruiting stock is grown. Buy only from a reputable dealer.

Here are some recommended varieties. Blackberry: 'Himalaya Giant', 'Johan Innes', 'Merton Thornless'. Raspberry: 'Glen Clover', 'Lloyd George', 'Malling Admiral', 'September'. Loganberry: virus-free 'LY 59', thornless 'L 654'.

Once planted blackberry canes should be shortened to about 3 ft and tied to their supports. In spring when the plants are beginning to grow shorten to about 10 ins above ground level cutting above a strong bud. To prune, cut-out old canes and tie in the new ones to bear fruit the next season.

With loganberries cut back after planting to encourage strong basal growth. Tie them into place. Thornless loganberries can be grown if preferred.

Raspberry fruit should not be picked in the first year but the suckers from below ground will bear fruit the next season. Support to prevent canes snapping. Once picking has finished cut out all fruited canes and tie in new ones to replace them. Remove all weak or small canes and allow about 5 new ones per stool.

Among the commonest pests and diseases that can attack your berries are aphids, raspberry beetle, cane blight, crown gall, grey mould, honey fungus and virus diseases. For methods of treatment consult the chapter in this book headed 'Pests and Diseases'.

RUBUS fruticosus
Blackberry

Description: The wild or common blackberry is the standard form of the European blackberry. Without support this variety will reach a height of 5 ft. Each fruit is in fact a collection of tiny fruits containing pips on one stem. At first the fruit is green; it then turns red and later black. As well as the wild bramble, there is also a large variety of cultivated blackberries. One of the most popular is 'Himalaya', a variety of the Rubus discolor. This is basically a self-pollinating type that bears large round or conical fruit. As well as the thorny European types of blackberry, there are also the thornless American varieties which are becoming increasingly popular. Most of these are of the Rubus laciniatus variety, with the 'Thornless Evergreen' being particularly good: the fruit is slightly larger than that of the 'Himalaya' and has a fine flavour, while the bush is less sensitive to stem disease and fruit rot. It is also winter hard, unlike the 'Himalaya'.

Care: Blackberries grow in good moisture retaining but well-drained soil. Stable manure must be dug in to the ground every year. They prefer to be grown as a hedge supported by poles and wires. The bushes flower from June to September. Although most blackberries are basically self-pollinating, cross-pollination is recommended. The fruit forms on the older wood. After harvesting, these fruit bearing branches die off. Propagation of the thorny European varieties is done by layering in autumn. By February-March, the layered shoots have rooted and are ready for transplanting. The American varieties cannot be layered because the root shoots have thorns. They are propagated by taking cuttings in summer and putting these into a mixture of peat and sand. Make sure that the atmosphere is kept very moist and that the temperature is a constant 20°C. If shoots with thorns should form, cut them off immediately otherwise they will take over. When planting blackberries it is a good idea to fill the holes with peat or pot soil, and to use this or stable manure for filling the gaps around the plants. This helps them to get established.

Harvesting: When the fruit is black. In a cold autumn, not all the fruit will ripen.

Preserving: Jam, syrup.

RUBUS idaeus
Raspberry

Description: For the space that they occupy they are more productive than any other fruit except strawberries. A hardy, deciduous cane.
Care: There are two kinds: summer-fruiting that produce fruit on the previous season's shoots, and the lighter-cropping autumn varieties. Sunny, protected site in moisture retaining, well-drained soil. Buy certified disease-free one-year old canes. Set in trench 9 ins wide and 3 ins deep 18 ins apart. Space rows 6 ft apart. Cut down each cane to 12 ins above soil. Mulch each April. Stake in summer.
Harvesting: When well-coloured all over.
Preserving: Bottled, frozen.

RUBUS loganobaccus
Loganberry

Description: Hardy perennial plant a cross between the blackberry and raspberry.
Care: Cut back canes, after planting, to a bud 9 ins above ground, mulch. Train loganberries along wires 12 ins apart and with top wire about 6 ft above ground. Each plant will need a good 12 ft span. Like raspberries, loganberries fruit best on canes developed the previous summer. After fruiting cut back to ground level the canes which bore fruit. Feed in January with sulphate of potash and in April with sulphate of ammonia.
Harvesting: Ripen in August, pick when juicy.
Preserving: Bottled, frozen.

RUBUS phoenicolasus
Wineberry

Description: Also known as the Japanese wine-berry, this is an attractive fruiting plant which boasts bright orange fruit turning to rich crimson when ripe. They have a slightly acidic flavour. The plant is less common than most varieties of berry.
Care: It grows to a height of about 8 ft with a spread of some 10 ft. Plant between October and March in fertile soil in sun or part shade. Can be trained against a wall. Dress annually with sulphate of potash in winter and sulphate of ammonia in March at 0.5 oz per square yard.
Harvesting: Ripen in August.
Preserving: Bottled, frozen.

SAMBUCUS nigra
Elder

Description: An attractive tree growing to 15 ft. Elderflower wine and elderberry wine are among the best home-brewed drinks.
Care: Plant in any fertile garden soil between October and March and then just leave it. It will prosper and more than likely need cutting back regularly. It can be prone to dense colonies of aphids, however, and in spring arabic mosaic virus may discolour the leaves.
Harvesting: Flowers in June, berries in September. To save time gather whole sprays rather than cutting individual berries.
Preserving: Bottled.

VACCINIUM corymbosum
Blueberry

Description: Hardy, deciduous, with blue-black berries.
Care: They thrive in acidic, peaty soil where many other plants will not grow. Need plenty of moisture and a soil with organic material well dug in. Plant in an open, sunny position between October and March in sun or part shade. Prune regularly to maintain a height of about 6 ft. Propagate by layering or by division between October and March, replanting in permanent position.
Harvesting: Let fruit mature on the bushes. Ripe when dark blue. Reddish tinges indicate immaturity.
Preserving: Bottled, frozen.

VACCINIUM macrocarpon
Cranberry

Description: A hardy, flat, wiry-stemmed shrub grown largely for its globular red berries which are cultivated commercially for the manufacture of cranberry sauce.
Care: Thrives in moisture retaining, peaty soil in an open position. Plant between October and March. It can be propagated by layering or by division between October and March. Sow seeds in cold frame in October in two parts peat one part sand, prick off when large enough to handle and grow in nursery bed for 3 years.
Harvesting: Gather when just ripe.
Preserving: Bottled, frozen, in sauce.

VACCINIUM myrtillus
Bilberry (blue)

Description: A deciduous hardy shrub of the same family as the blueberry and which bears blue-black fruit in July and August.
Care: It should thrive in good, moisture retaining peaty soil and an open spot. Plant between October and March either in sun or partial shade and make sure that the soil has been deeply dug and well manured. This is a long-lived shrub and looking after its needs will pay dividends. Propagate by layering in September or division between October and March. Can be sown from seed in a cold frame.
Harvesting: In July and August when newly ripe.
Preserving: Bottled, frozen.

VACCINIUM vitis-idaea
Cowberry, mountain cranberry, red bilberry

Description: A fairly flat evergreen species common to the mountain ranges of the Northern Temperate Zone. It grows up to 6 ins, spreads up to 18 ins and bears white or pale pink flowers in one inch long racenes in May and June. Fruit are dark red, globular berries about 0.5 long. The berries follow the flowers and may well carry on into the winter.
Care: Growing methods and soil preparation are the same as for other vacciniums.
Harvesting: When fruit is newly ripe.
Preserving: Bottled or frozen.

VITIS vinifera
Grape

Introduction

Grapes have been grown for centuries. The Romans brought them to northern Europe and made wine from them, as did the ancient Greeks.

In those parts of Europe where wine-making is a tradition and a profitable business the cultivation of grapes is talked about as though it was a mystic art. To hear wine buffs talk you might think that growing grapes was best left to a small group of experts whose skills were born of centuries of knowledge passed from father to son. In fact the Americans have successfully debunked that myth by producing splendid wine grapes in California by dull, but scientific, methods. No magic is needed – just warmth and common-sense. Given good weather and by following the growing advice it should be quite possible to grow your own grapes whether you want them for eating or to press to make one or two bottles of your own wine.

In the last few years there has been a big revival in the cultivation of grapes and more and more summerhouses, greenhouses and sunny pergolas boast the splendid climbing foliage and bursting white and red fruit.

The grape-vine is a sturdy deciduous climber but although hardy it needs a long warm summer for the fruit to ripen and in these climes will be more successful under some sort of glass protection. If it is to be grown out of doors then it will be important to plant it in areas which tend to have milder weather and on a south-facing slope free from spring frosts. Those living in northerly regions will find it difficult to achieve any significant results. Vines are self-fertile but cross-pollination is a good idea. Plant any two varieties which flower at the same time. If growing under glass then artificial pollination with a camel hair brush may be necessary.

Outdoor varieties: chiefly for wine-making, 'Reisling Sylvaner' or 'Siegerrebe'. Indoor varieties: 'Black Hamburgh' is probably the best-known and most commonly grown and has large sweet fruit; 'Buckland Sweetwater' with medium, green, juicy berries or 'Alicante' with large, black fruit.

Pests which attack grapes include: glasshouse red spider mites, mealy bugs and scale insects. Diseases include grey mould, honey fungus, mildew, magnesium deficiency and scald.

VITIS vinifera
Climbing grape vine

Description: The simplest way of growing grapes is to plant a climbing variety like 'Black Hamburgh' or 'Buckland Sweetwater' which can be trained up a wall, fence or pergola.

Care: Plant the vine in the same way as we described for outdoor grown grapes, setting them about 4 ft apart and leaving some 9 ins between the plant and the wall or fence. The method involves training the vine on a single cordon or rod. Select the strongest leader to grow as the rod and cut out the others to one bud. Tie the leader to a firmly buried cane securing the cane to the wires which are tied in the same fashion as for open growing, except that wires are attached to the wall. In the following growing season, as the flowers begin to appear, pinch them out and in the middle to late August cut back the laterals to 4-5 leaves. In November cut out the immature wood on the stem going back to ripe, mature wood brown in colour and not less than pencil thick. In the second year repeat the process but in the summer also cut back the sub-laterals to one leaf. You should by now have produced a cordon which is well-spurred and capable of providing a modest harvest the following fruiting season.

Allow only three bunches to each cordon in the first cropping year and in the second increase this to about five bunches per cordon. After this keep cropping to a rate of one bunch to each foot run. In a good year a cordon grown against a wall or fence could produce as much as 15 lbs of grapes. Keep the ground well-watered, particularly in the year after planting. In the spring mulch the ground along the rows with peat or well-rotted compost. In February dress each side of the row with a good general fertiliser at the rate of 1.5-2 oz per square yard. In April give the soil a top dressing of magnesium sulphate at the rate of around 1.5-2 oz per square yard.

Harvesting: The grapes will be ready for harvesting when they begin to change colour. For black grapes this will be more obvious than for green ones. Do not pluck the grapes from the vine since this can cause damage. Cut with scissors. They should keep in a cool place for about two months after picking.

Preserving: Bottled, dried, wine.

VITIS vinifera
Glasshouse grown grapes

Description: A number of varieties are best suited to growing under glass. They include 'Black Hamburgh' and 'Alicante'.
Care: Plant two-year-old vines in October to February either in pots of potting compost or in rich fertile soil made up to ten parts loam to one of crushed brick, which has been enriched with fertiliser, bone meal and dried blood. Before planting you will need to set up a wire network of supports 12 ins apart and held 18 ins from the roof. Single rods or cordons can reach a height of 20 ft with a 3 ft spread so plan for this. Set out pot-grown plants in late autumn or winter spaced about 4 ft apart. Train the plants against the wires running along the greenhouse. Water the plants copiously to promote as much growth as possible during the first season but only allow one stem to develop. In the autumn as the leaves change colour remove about half of the growth from the first year rods. Select a bud on well-ripened wood and cut back to it. When spring arrives train the leading shoot upwards and the lateral shoots horizontally both ways. After flowering stop the laterals at two leaves beyond the fruit clusters and any subsequent shoots at one leaf. Only allow about 2-3 fruit bunches to set in the first cropping year rubbing out all other shoots.
In the autumn cut back about half of the new growth to the well-ripened wood on the leading rod. Cut back the main rod and lateral shoots for two years to fill up and to build strong and sturdy fruit spurs. In the winter ventilate and allow some frost into the greenhouse. Scrub the rods gently, while they are dormant, with a tar-oil winter wash. Ventilate until about March. In April close ventilators in order to increase the temperature and induce buds to break. Spray copiously with water twice daily. The buds should swell rapidly. Select the strongest shoot from each spur rubbing out the others with the thumb. In about two weeks select the best with the longest flowering trusses. Stop these at two leaves beyond the bunch pinching out the others at the fourth leaf. In May, when the flowers open, pollinate with a camel hair brush. Keep temperature high and humidity low until flowers have set, then ventilate. As berries swell, thin gradually over 1-2 weeks. Keep watering until colour shows in fruit. Stop liquid feed.
Harvesting: September to October.
Preserving: Dried, bottled, wine.

VITIS vinifera
Grapes grown outdoors

Description: Generally speaking the earlier-ripening varieties should be chosen. Most outdoor varieties are best grown for wine. Try 'Sylvaner Reisling' or 'Seyve Villard' which can also be eaten as a dessert grape.
Care: Plant the vines at any time when they are dormant, usually between October and March. Plant in a sheltered position ideally on a south-facing slope in full sun. Avoid any frost pockets. The best soil will be sandy so that it warms up quickly in sun. To promote better drainage, which is critical, dig a 2 ft deep trench leading away from the vine, cover the bottom with brick rubble and, three months before planting, dig in well-rotted manure. Set stakes 5 ft high and 8 ft apart with 5 ft between rows. Attach a length of galvanised wire 18 ins from the ground. Next attach two lengths of wire twisted together 2.5 ft above ground level and another length of twisted wires 18 ins above that. To plant, dig a hole wide enough for the roots and deep enough to take the vine at the same level it was in the nursery. Sink a supporting cane for each vine so that 6 ft is above ground. Plant the vines 4 ft apart.
In the first year allow only the strongest shoot to grow, pinching out all others at two leaves. In November start to train the vines. Cut down to about four buds. The following summer allow the three strongest shoots to grow, pinching out the rest. In November tie two shoots laterally along bottom wire, cutting back the third to three buds. The following summer train the fruiting laterals on horizontal stems through the double wires. In August cut the tops of the laterals to three leaves above the top wire. Remove the sub-laterals. Tie the three replacement shoots to the cane and pinch back their laterals to one leaf. In November remove the two shoots carrying the fruiting laterals. Tie two replacement shoots to the bottom wire. Cut back the third to three buds. Repeat this process each year. This is the Guyot system of training. In the first fruiting year restrict crop to four bunches, in the second six bunches and then allow a full crop. Keep ground well-watered and mulch the rows with peat or compost each spring. In Feb apply general fertiliser along each side of rows. In April top dress with magnesium sulphate.
Harvesting: When they change colour.
Preserving: Bottled, dried, wine.

VEGETABLES, GUIDE FOR SOWING AND HARVESTING

In the following guide for sowing and harvesting vegetables you will find the most common vegetables listed. Some sorts do not have a fixed sowing and harvesting period because these periods change per variety or because these sorts can be grown throughout the year. These vegetables are indicated with a note. Consult the central listing or the instructions on the seedbag for more detailed information about sowing and harvesting periods.

	jan	feb	mar	apr	may	jun	jul	aug	sep	oct	nov	dec
Allium ascalonicum **Shallot**												
Allium cepa* **Onion**												
Allium porrum* **Leek**												
Apium graveolens var. dulce **Self blanching celery**												
Apium graveolens var. rapaceum **Celeriac**												
Apium graveolens var. secalinum **Celery**												
Beta vulgaris **Beetroot**												
Beta vulgaris var. cicla† **Spinach Beet**												
Brassica cernua **Chinese cabbage**												
Brassica napus **Swede**												
Brassica oleracea var. acephale laciniata **Kale**												
Brassica oleracea var. botrytis cauliflora* **Cauliflower**												
Brassica oleracea var. botrytis cymosa **Broccoli**												
Brassica oleracea var. bullata gemmifera **Brussels sprouts**												
Brassica oleracea var. bullata sabauda† **Savoy cabbage**												
Brassica oleracea var. capitata alba* **White cabbage**												
Brassica oleracea var. capitata conica **Oxheart cabbage**												
Brassica oleracea var. capitata rubra **Red cabbage**												
Brassica oleracea var. gogylodes† **Kohl rabi**												
Brassica pabularia* **Turnip-tops**												
Brassica rapa* **Turnip**												
Cichorium endivia* **Endive**												
Cichorium intybus **Green chicory**												
Cichorium intybus **Chicory**												
Claytonia perforliata **Winter purslane**												
Cucumis sativus† **Gherkin**												

VEGETABLES, GUIDE FOR SOWING AND HARVESTING

	jan	feb	mar	apr	may	jun	jul	aug	sep	oct	nov	dec
Cucumis sativus **Cucumber**			▓	▓			■	■				
Cucurbita maxima **Pumpkin**				▓								
Cucurbita pepo **Gourd**				▒	▒	▒	■					
Cynara scolymus **Globe artichoke**		■	■	▒					■			
Daucus carota* **Carrot**												
Foeniculum dulce **Florence fennel**				■					▒	■		
Lactuca sativa* **Lettuce**												
Lepidium sativum† **Cress**												
Phaseolus coccineus **Runnerbean**						■			■			
Phaseolus vulgaris* **French beans**												
Pisum sativum* **Peas**												
Portulaca sativa **Purslane**					▒	■	■					
Raphanus sativus var. radicula* **Radish**												
Rheum rhaponticum **Rhubarb**			▒	■	■					▒		
Scorzonera hispanica **Scorzonera**	■	■		■	■						■	■
Solanum lycopersicum* **Tomato**												
Solanum tuberosum* **Potato**												
Solanum melongena **Aubergine**		■							■	■		
Spinacia oleracea* **Spinach**												
Stachys affinis var. tubifera **Chinese artichoke**			▒	▒								■
Valerianella locusta† **Corn salad**												
Vicia faba **Broad bean**				▒			■					
Zea mays **Sweet corne**				▒	▒			■				

* dependent on variety
† dependent on desired harvesting date

▓ sowing in boxes/pots/etc.

☐ sowing on the spot

▒ planting

■ harvesting

Fruit, guide for harvesting

In the following guide for harvesting fruit, you will find the most common fruit listed. Because most fruit grow on older trees, we have not mentioned sowing periods on this list. Information about sowing and planting you will find in the individual listings.

	Jan	Febr	March	April	May	June	July	Aug	Sept	Oct	Nov	Dec
Apple									●	●	●	
Bilberry							●	●				
Blackberry							●	●	●	●		
Cherry						●	●	●				
Currant						●	●	●				
Elder									●			
Fig								●	●			
Gooseberry					●	●	●	●				
Hothouse grape									●	●		
Loganberry								●				
Peach							●	●				
Pear									●	●		
Plum								●	●			
Quince										●		
Raspberry								●	●	●		
Sea buckthorne	●	●								●	●	●
Strawberry					●	●	●	●	●	●		
Sweet chestnut										●	●	
Wineberry							●	●				

Vegetables, crop-combination: successive on the same spot or in the near vicinity

When you have a small garden, you will want to use the available ground as good as possible. It is possible to grow different crops in one year on the same spot or in the near vicinity. This is called crop-combination. Some crops have a favourable or unfavourable influence on one another. It is advisable to keep this in mind, when planning the vegetable-garden. In the following schedule you will find the most common vegetables.

● = favourable for growth, health and taste.
○ = unfavourable

	Bean	Beet-root	Cab-bage	Carrot	Cucum-ber	Leek	Lettuce	Onion	Pea	Radish	Spi-nach	Tomato
Bean		○	●	●	●	○	●	○	●	●		
Beetroot	○		●			●		●				
Cabbage	●	●				●	●	●	●	○	●	●
Carrot	●					●	●	●	●	●		●
Cucumber	●					●			●	○		○
Leek	○	●		●				●	○			●
Lettuce	●		●	●				●	●	●		
Onion	○	●	●			●	●		○	●		●
Pea	●		●	●	●	○	●	○		●		
Radish	●		○	●	○		●	●	●			
Spinach			●									
Tomato			●	●	○	●		●				

Fruit, pollination

The production of good crops of fruit depends on pollination and fertilisation. Many sorts require cross-pollination, if they are to set good crops. Other sorts are self-fertile. With these trees though, cropping is improved if other pollinators of the same kind of fruit are in the near vicinity.

	self-pollination	cross-pollination
Apple		●
Kiwi fruit		●
Pear		●
Plum	●	
Sea buckthorn		●
Strawberry		●
Vine	●	

Vegetables, preserving

In the following schedule you will find a short summary of the possible ways of preserving vegetables. Those vegetables that are not listed, are best eaten fresh.

	Bottle	Deep-freeze	Cool in boxes/earth
Asparagus	●	●	
Aubergine		●	
Beetroot	●	●	●
Black radish			●
Broad bean	●	●	
Broccoli		●	
Brussels sprouts	●	●	
Carrots		●	
Cauliflower	●	●	
Celeriac			●
Celery	●	●	
Chinese artichoke			●
Cucumber	●		
Florence fennel		●	
Gherkin	●		
Globe artichoke		●	
Green chicory			●
Kohl rabi		●	
Leek		●	
Lentils			●
Marrow	●	●	
Melon	●	●	
Parsnip			●
Pepper	●	●	
Pickling onion	●		
Potato		●	
Pumpkin	●		●
Radish			●
Red cabbage	●	●	

	Bottle	Deep-freeze	Cool in boxes/earth
Red pepper*	●		
Rhubarb	●	●	
Runner bean		●	
Scorzonera			●
Self blanching celery	●	●	
Shallot	●	●	
Soya bean			●
Spinach		●	
Sugar pea		●	
Swede			●
Sweet corn	●	●	
Tomato	●		
Turnip		●	●
Winter carrot			●

* can also be dried

Fruit, preserving

Fruit is mostly eaten fresh. You can even prepare the most delicious juices, if you have a juice-making machine. Fruit can also be preserved for a longer period though some preparation is needed in this case.
Information about preserving is contained in a special section in this book; more detailled information about the preparation is best found in a cookery-book. In the following schedule you will find a short summary of the possible ways of preserving fruit. Fruit not listed, is best eaten fresh.

	dry	freeze	bottle	cook	syrup	wine	jam/jelly	mash
apple	●	●	●					●
apricot	●	●	●		●		●	●
berry		●	●				●	
cherry (sweet)		●	●				●	
cherry (acid)			●				●	
currant		●	●				●	
damson			●			●		
elder			●				●	
fig	●		●					
grape	●		●			●		
kiwi fruit			●				●	
medlar			●				●	
mulberry	●	●	●					●
nectarine		●	●		●			●
peach	●	●	●		●			●
pear	●	●	●	●				●
plum	●	●	●	●	●		●	●
quince		●		●				
raspberry		●	●		●		●	
rosehip					●		●	
sea buckthorne							●	
strawberry		●	●		●		●	●
sweet chestnut			●	●				●
walnut	●		●					

INDEX

INDEX

The pictures in this book were supplied by:

Frans Brugman: pg. 2, 7, 11, 12, 13, 18, 21, 29, 31;

Tjerk Buishand: pg. 37(ra), 39(ra), 39(rb), 44(rb), 45(ra), 45(lb), 47(la), 48(ra), 48(lb), 50(lb), 51(ra), 52(ra), 59(lb), 60(lb), 60(rb), 66(rb), 74(rb);

Centraal Bureau van de Tuinbouwveilingen in Nederland, The Hague (Netherlands): pg. 74(la), 78(ra), 79(la);

Instituut voor de Veredeling van Tuinbouwgewassen, Wageningen (Netherlands): pg. 23, 32, 42(la), 49, 69(rb), 70(lb), 71(ra), 74(lb), 75(lb), 75(rb), 78(la), 78(lb), 79(rb);

Paul Pet: pg. 76;

Proefstation voor de Fruitteelt, Wilhelminadorp (Netherlands): pg. 63(ra), 64(ra), 64(lb), 66(ra), 68(la), 79(ra), 79(lb), 84(ra), 84(rb);

Vakgroep Tropische Plantenteelt, Wageningen (Netherlands): pg. 48(rb), 52(rb);

Willemse, Hillegom (Netherlands): pg. 63(lb), 63(rb), 64(rb), 66(lb), 67, 68(lb), 69(la), 69(ra), 70(la), 70(ra), 71(lb), 71(rb), 72, 73, 74(ra), 75(la), 81(lb), 82(la), 82(ra), 83(lb), 85(la), 85(ra), 86(ra).

All other pictures come from the archives of Fleurmerc, Wormerveer (Netherlands).

la = left above; lb = left below; ra = right above; rb = right below.